Rock Garden Plants

A Hamlyn Colour Guide

Rock Garden Plants

by **Vlasta Vodičková**

Illustrated by
Jiřina Kaplická

Hamlyn

London • New York • Sydney • Toronto

Translated by Dana Hábová
Graphic design by František Prokeš
Designed and produced by Artia for
The Hamlyn Publishing Group Limited
London ● New York ● Sydney ● Toronto
Astronaut House, Feltham, Middlesex, England

ISBN 0 600 30555 4
Printed in Czechoslovakia
3/15/10/51—01

CONTENTS

The attraction of a rock garden   7

Materials   8

Choice of site   8

Building a rock garden   9

Plants for the rock garden   11

Shrubs and trees   12

Colour illustrations   15

Some facts about ecology   209

Maintenance and care   210

Paths and steps   211

Water in the rock garden   212

The bog garden, alpine meadow and scree bed   214

The sink garden   215

Dry stone walls   216

Keeping a record of your plants   218

Bibliography   219

Index   221

THE ATTRACTION OF A ROCK GARDEN

Constructing a rock garden has become very popular. Some people build it simply for show, while for others it can be a delightful and interesting hobby. The rock garden itself will show, all in good time, to what category its owner belongs. A true enthusiast does not build the rock garden as a status symbol, but will work happily in his spare time away from the daily rush of life. And though his garden may not be perfect, it makes a lovely sight because it is well kept, and the plants repay the care and love lavished on them. The construction of the rock garden is only the beginning of work. The rock gardener need never be bored as there is always something to be done throughout the year. In winter, the gardener studies gardening books and catalogues to get to know his plants, and plans any changes to parts of the rock garden which does not quite satisfy him. Then, all of a sudden, the winter is over and the first blossoms welcome the spring.

In spring, we worry about the more delicate species and see how they survived the winter (no winter is too mild for the rock gardener), or what damage has been done by mice and other uninvited visitors. In summer we decide where to plant the bulbs of the new varieties and species of tulips, daffodils or squills, and what dwarf conifers or deciduous shrubs we have to get to fill the gaps in and around the rock garden. In autumn we set out these new bulbs and imagine their beautiful flowers emerging in spring.

Rock gardening is a wonderful but insidious hobby. If you take it up, you are lost! For 365 days a year you will be busy working in your rock garden or wishing you could. You will take trips to specialist nurseries and bring home some new plants, and beg some more from friends who share your hobby. You will soon find that your rock garden is not big enough; then realize you have not enough room for the alpine meadow or scree bed which you desperately need for the new plants you want to grow. And you will come to the conclusion that the rockery has to be enlarged.

The rock garden represents an individual's creative work and since the result may often be disappointing in comparison with your ideal, you will have many reasons to go on improving and rearranging the rockery. Constant creative activity and constant change are the basic attributes of the rock gardener.

MATERIALS

To build the rock garden, you will need not only stone but also gravel, sand, peat, loam, leafmould and moss peat (*Sphagnum*). In addition to the building material, every rock gardener needs immense patience, perseverance and naturally a great love of plants.

If possible, use a local stone for the construction; preferably choosing weathered slabs. Fresh stone from a quarry is not suitable as it will make the rock garden look unnatural. A rock garden is not a geological exhibition so only one kind of stone should be used. If you have a large rock garden, made of granite or limestone, you could build an independent section from sandstone, peat or some other material if you so wish. However, the two kinds of stone should never be mixed in one rock garden. Sandstone is porous and holds water well. It can be both alkaline or acid, depending on the mineral content of the cementing material.

The basic construction materials also include gravel, which is used as drainage material. Fine gravel is used to top dress round the stems of some plants to protect them from excessive moisture. The gravel can be limestone, granite or lime-free rock chippings. Gravel provides the basic material for a scree bed.

Sand should be a sharp sand or preferably a river-washed sand, clean and without clay particles. This is used to lighten the soil, especially heavy clays. It is applied in a larger quantity to plants requiring a poor, sandy soil such as *Draba*. Various mixtures of compost will include loam or rotted turves, leafmould, silver sand and peat. Loam is the basic material which is combined with various other ingredients according to the requirements of specific plants. For instance rhododendrons need a large amount of peat and coarse pine needles added, the Lady's Slipper orchid benefits from beech leafmould, and *Gentiana verna* appreciates extra moss peat. Mountain plants are undemanding and must not be planted in well-manured soil. Other species flourish in soil improved with a little bonemeal. Artificial fertilizers are used sparingly. Only bulbous and tuberous plants can be fed more heavily to form strong underground bodies capable of flowering.

CHOICE OF SITE

Plan the site of the rock garden carefully. A large area is not required as even a small rockery can accommodate a number of small rock garden plants, as can be seen in raised scree beds, sink and trough gardens. Choose an airy and sunny situation in a place where your rockery can be viewed from a distance. It can be surrounded by a well-tended lawn with two or three boulders and a prominent solitary plant, a columnar conifer or deciduous shrub, or a tall herbaceous plant such as *Eremurus, Cortaderia,* or a mullein. The background is equally important; a wall of dark green yews or other conifers looks most effective.

If you are lucky enough to have some free space or have just acquired a virgin plot you can carry out more of your artistic ideas and plans than in an established garden that has already been laid out with trees and flower beds. You should plan to construct a small greenhouse if possible or at least a cold frame for propagating new plants.

Sloping ground is most advantageous, although an attractive rock garden can also be built on flat ground. You can either heap up soil and model it, or dig out an irregular hole and build a flatter rock garden, or combine both these approaches. Never forget to make the rock garden look natural even on flat ground. Besides rock gardens which resemble a natural environment, there are also dry wall gardens which are suitable for modern houses. This type of garden for alpine plants will be described in more detail later.

Every beginner makes mistakes and it is advisable to do some reading about rock gardening and try to visit any noted rock gardens in your area. Do not be afraid to chat to any friends you have who have created a successful rockery. By getting to know various types of rock gardens, you can learn the practicalities as well as getting plenty of ideas. You will be able to plan your own future rock garden and as soon as this is complemented by the knowledge of the methods of construction you can begin to build.

BUILDING A ROCK GARDEN

After selecting the site and establishing the ground plan of the rock garden, you can start the construction. First of all clean up the area by lifting and stacking the turf and digging out all perennial weeds which could later become troublesome. If possible, choose an eastern, north-eastern or south-eastern exposure as these are best for most mountain species. Only a few species can be successfully grown in a south- or west-facing rock garden. Start by heaping builder's rubble, broken bricks or gravel for underlying drainage material, because most alpine plants will not tolerate waterlogged ground. If you have clay soil which tends to be wet, the drainage layer must be much thicker, 20 in (50 cm) at least than in more freely-draining soil. Cover the gravel base with soil well mixed with loam or chopped turves, sharp sand, peat and leafmould. Alpine plants either do not produce flowers or become too tall and the foliage too sparse in very rich soil.

If you are planning to build a larger rockery, make a preliminary layout of paths and steps, and lay down the foundation stones for these in a bedding of sand. The rockery should give the impression of a natural landscape. The ground should be divided into hollows, platforms, peaks and sloping ground. There should be parts that are exposed to direct sunshine as well as shaded areas out of the sun, to enable the cultivation of plants with different ecological requirements.

The stones are embedded deeply in the modelled ground, so that only the top third is exposed and they look like jutting outcrops (1). Always lay the stones on their broadest side, beginning at the lowest sections of the rock garden. You can make joints, slopes or vertical walls as you go. Irregular patches can be formed both on horizontal and sloping ground. Regularity in a rock garden looks unnatural, and the stones should vary in size and be arranged in irregular rows. Any

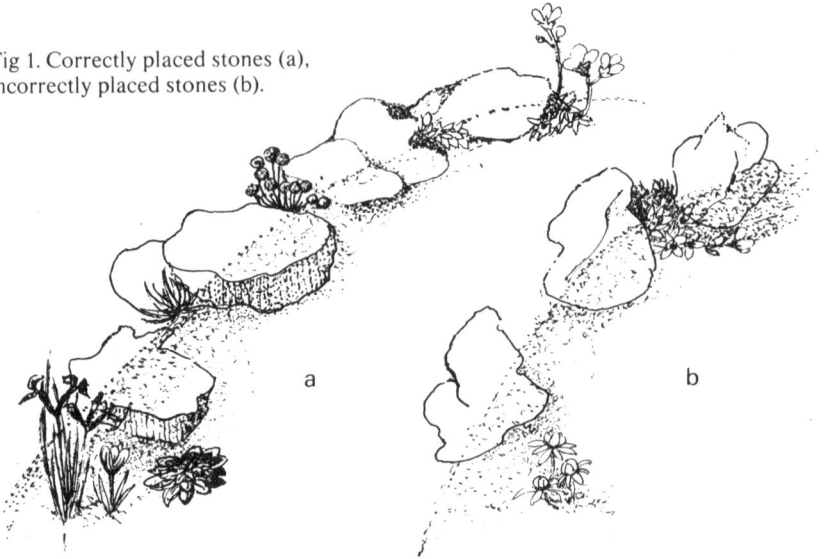

Fig 1. Correctly placed stones (a), incorrectly placed stones (b).

a

b

boulders found in the countryside should be placed in their natural position and the strata should align. The finished rockery should look well even without plants. Never copy your neighbour's garden, but look to nature for inspiration, with its genuine rocky crevices, patches of soil between stones or screes. Draw your ideas from a natural boggy area or a solitary stone outcrop; observe well.

For some months, preferably a year or over winter, leave the rock garden unplanted to let the soil settle. Seeds of weeds in the ground will sprout by this time, and then the garden can be given another thorough clearing before planting. Some more soil should be added to fill any gaps in between the stones and then the plants set out.

PLANTS FOR THE ROCK GARDEN

When the rock garden is finished, you can start another pleasant, interesting and creative job — setting out the plants. Never take the plants from the wild. In Great Britain and most other European countries, the upland regions have become national parks and all the plants in them enjoy protection. Many lowland plants are also endangered and are protected. Experienced rock gardeners can cultivate the species which have almost disappeared from natural sites, and in this way contribute to their safeguard. Some ruthless people pick the plants from their natural, often depleted habitats, for profit. No gardener should follow their example. Alpine plants obtained from specialized nurseries give the best guarantee that you get precisely what you order. You can get other plants or cuttings from friends who have succeeded in growing the wild 'beauties' of mountain and countryside from seed. Such plants are much hardier and better withstand adverse conditions, unsuitable for many other species.

When working on the layout of a new rock garden, your possibilities are boundless. You may think you have so much space you can buy any plant you like. But you will soon discover that there is not room for everything. It takes strategic planning and perhaps even some transplanting before finding the right spot. You make a resolution not to buy another plant, but in vain. In time, you will simply have to enlarge your rock garden if you can. If you have plenty of space, it is best to build as large a rock garden as you can to begin with. In this case the selection of plants will offer more possibilities. A large rock garden can be divided into vegetational complexes: e. g. alpine flora from New Zealand, from European mountains, from

North America or from the Himalayas. You will not produce the best effect by mixing species from New Zealand (e. g. *Celmisia, Raoulia*) with the European snowbreads or the Himalayan pleiones.

The plants are set out so that certain areas of the rockery flower at different periods to produce a colourful, harmonious effect throughout the year. Avoid a combination of four pink-flowered plants blooming at the same time. Never place tall plants at the top of the rockery, but only in the lower areas at the sides. Still, no matter how carefully you study the flowering periods and habitats of plants, errors will happen. The following season after planting will reveal that the pink *Dianthus microlepis* is in the wrong spot and all that is left from the beautiful, spring-flowering *Pulsatilla vulgaris* is a massive tuft of leaves completely shading the small Whitlow Grass or the Rockrose which needs full sun. You will see that *Helichrysum milfordiae* is spreading wonderfully but lacks space, and because you find it attractive, you have to transplant all the plants in its vicinity. All this means constant change, but increases the rock gardener's knowledge and curiosity about the next season.

SHRUBS AND TREES

Shrubs and trees are indispensable for dividing the rock garden into sections and provide a background to the low-growing plants. Careful planning before setting out the woody plants is most important. The final size has to be considered to avoid transplanting mature shrubs or trees, which is always difficult in a rock garden. Preference is given to low-growing, stunted species and cultivars of which there is a wide assortment among conifers and deciduous trees and shrubs. Most conifers are evergreen and remain attractive throughout the winter and should be present in every rock garden. They include the dwarf pine, *Pinus mugo,* or the smaller *P. m. pumilio.* In small rock gardens, the trees can be restricted in their growth by nipping back the new growth tips in spring. Some Juniper cultivars are also suitable. One of the smallest columnar ones is *Juniperus communis* 'Compressa' which can be situated in a very small rockery. The creeping *Juniperus procumbens* 'Nana' makes a dark green cover to the ground and stones. Other low-growing conifers are the spruce *Picea glauca* 'Echiniformis' with short, silvery needles and a maximum height of 1 ft (30 cm). The beautiful, spherically shaped fir *Abies balsamea* 'Hudsonia' is slightly taller. Other low conifers are mostly cultivars of the genera *Thuja, Chamaecyparis* and *Tsuga.* Larger rockeries are often planted with *Picea glauca* 'Conica', the slow-growing Cypress *Chamaecyparis obtusa* 'Nana Gracilis', *Tsuga canadensis* 'Jeddeloh' and others.

There is also a wide range of deciduous woody plants suitable for rock gardens. Among the best-known and most frequently cultivated is the *Cotoneaster*. There are both deciduous and evergreen species, from large to quite small shrubs, providing suitable subjects for any type of rock garden. For very small rockeries choose one of the small, ornamental species, *C. microphyllus* or *C. dammeri* var. *radicans* with tiny, rounded leaves, which grows over the ground and stones. The evergreen *C. congestus* and the similar, although deciduous *C. adpressus* are also handsome. The well-known *C. horizontalis* reaches dimensions which make it suited only for very large rock gardens. Some small species of willow trees should not be absent from rock gardens. Those thriving in cultivation include even some high-mountain, creeping species such as *Salix retusa, S. herbacea* and, one of the prettiest, *S. reticulata,* a slow-grower recommended for small rock gardens but sometimes doing poorly in cultivation. The well-known creeping woody plants of low growth include the Mountain Avens, with its ornamental flowers, foliage and fruits. There are a number of species of broom, producing a wealth of usually bright yellow flowers. Some brooms are low, creeping shrubs, others attain a height of 6 ft (2 m) and have a beautiful habit and large flowers. The lowest growing species include *Cytisus decumbens,* the profusely flowering *C.* × *kewensis* and *C. purpureus* are taller species. *C.* × *praecox* or *C. scoparius* can be used in large rock gardens or as solitary plants. The Barberry is another woody plant to be recommended. *Berberis thunbergii* 'Atropurpurea Nana' has ornamental, tiny, red-tinged leaves in the autumn, and another small species is the evergreen *B. candidula.* Many other species are available. Rhododendrons also exist in many species suitable for both small and larger rock gardens, and you can enjoy the massed effect of their magnificent flowers. Among the lowest growing ones are the deciduous *R. camtschaticum,* the evergreen *R. myrtilloides* or *R. keleticum. R. impeditum* and its cultivars are very rewarding and hardy.

There is not room here to list all the trees and shrubs suitable for the rock garden, but every rock gardener can choose from the wide assortment according to his needs and personal preferences.

COLOUR ILLUSTRATIONS

Acaenas are undemanding plants, easy to cultivate. Their trailing stems take root freely and spread to form ornamental mats. The leaves are persistent, alternate, pinnate with an unpaired terminal leaflet. Acaenas thrive in humus-rich soil, not too heavy and well drained. They are intolerant of situations which are either too moist or too dry. They grow both in the sun and in light shade, but the specimens planted in shady places develop long, thin, straggly growths.

All species of *Acaena* spread in carpets which can replace lawns or fill the gaps between stepping stones. They can mix well with heaths and heathers or can be grown on a dry wall. They can be set out in beds between bulbous plants which have finished flowering. Propagation is by division or by cutting of young shoots.

Some 60 species of *Acaena* are distributed mainly in the Southern Hemisphere, particularly in New Zealand, Australia, Tasmania, the Andes, Mexico, South America. New Zealand is the home of *A. microphylla* and the robust *A. novae-zelandiae,* which attains a height of 6 in (15 cm) or more. The shoots are over 3 ft (1 m) long and the plant requires a lot of space and grows best in partial shade.

The delicate *Acaena argentea* from South America has trailing stems and ornamental, leathery, silvery-blue leaves, hairy on the undersides.

Acaena microphylla (1) has rounded, deeply notched, brownish-green single leaflets. The tiny inconspicuous flowers are clustered in spherical inflorescences on thin stalks, about 2 in (5 cm) tall. A fruit-bearing specimen is more ornamental because the inflorescence is transformed into a bristly reddish-brown head about 1/2 in (1 cm) across.

Acaena glaucophylla (*A. magellanica)* (2), native to Patagonia, is more delicate. Its creeping reddish-coloured branches bear unpaired pinnate leaves of a blue-green colour, up to 4 in (10 cm) long, with rounded, deeply notched leaflets. The plant forms thin carpets 4 to 6 in (10 to 15 cm) high. The ornamental heads appear in August.

Acaena buchananii (3) has silvery-grey, slightly hairy leaves and is native to New Zealand. It is a low growing plant which forms thick carpets. The flowerheads are covered with yellow spines.

1

2

3

Prickly Thrift
Acantholimon glumaceum

The Prickly Thrift is a perennial evergreen plant with tough needle-like, prickly leaves, gradually spreading to form large cushions. It is indigenous to the plains and mountainsides of Armenia and Asia Minor. Only a few species of *Acantholimon* are cultivated in rock gardens.

The plants require a sheltered position in full sun and with good drainage. They do best in poor calcareous soil to which coarse sand and limestone gravel have been added. The most suitable situation is a rocky crevice. As they are sensitive to excessive moisture in the winter, they should be covered with glass throughout the rainy winter months. They hardly ever flower if their situation is unsuitable. Great care should be taken in setting out the plants initially because transplanting older specimens usually fails.

Acantholimons are propagated from the seed or from cuttings in July or August. The plants can also be lightly covered with soil in the autumn, and the stems which have taken root are separated in the spring. Grafting on to the roots of *Limonium* is also possible. The easiest method of propagation is by seed. These usually germinate well and should be sown as soon as they are ripe or in February. Unfortunately, acantholimons cultivated in gardens either form no seeds or the seeds do not germinate.

Acantholimon glumaceum (1) from Armenia is one of the hardiest and most frequently cultivated species. The leaves form a dark green ground rosette from which grows the stem, 3 to 3½ in (8 to 9 cm) tall, with a spiky inflorescence. The pink flowers appear in June and July, sometimes even in August. The fruits (2) are also ornamental.

Acantholimon olivieri, often mistaken for *A. venustum,* is native to Asia Minor. It forms dense and prickly blue-green cushions, pricklier than in *A. glumaceum.* It has a wealth of deep pink flowers. It is less resistant to cold and needs a dry sheltered position. It is a rare rock garden plant because it is difficult to propagate. The seeds germinate freely in the wild but are not formed in our climatic conditions, and the cuttings rarely send out roots.

1

2

Japanese Maple
Acer palmatum

Aceraceae

Maples are usually thought of as too large for a rock garden. But there are some slow-growing species, mostly of non-European origin, and at least one of them should be represented in the rock garden. These maples can be trimmed and there is no need to worry about their final size, which is about 6 to 13 ft (2 to 4 m). If there is plenty of space and suitable conditions in a large rock garden or its surroundings, these beautiful woody plants should be represented.

Two very impressive species are the *Acer japonicum* from Japan and *A. palmatum* originating from Japan, Korea and China. In their homeland, they form medium-tall trees or large bushes, but in European conditions they belong more among the shrubs. They are hardy but should, however, be planted in a sheltered spot in a position that highlights their fiery autumn coloration and fine shape. They are best propagated from seed, but can be grafted onto a rootstock of the same species as the scion.

Acer palmatum has fine, variable leaves, divided into five to eleven narrow, double-toothed lobes, and thin branches. The finer the leaves and branches are, the lower growing and more attractive the plant is. Two slow-growing cultivars are 'Atropurpureum' (3) with delicate bronzy crimson leaves assuming a fiery scarlet in autumn, and 'Atropurpureum Dissectum' (1) which has the same coloration but its leaves are even more finely divided and the extremely thin branches are slightly pendulous.

A beautifully coloured complementary plant for *Acer palmatum* 'Atropurpureum' is *A. palmatum japonicum* (2). The highly ornamental, rounded, double-toothed leaves have seven to eleven lobes and are a bright light green in summer turning red in autumn. The frequently grown cultivar 'Aureum' is a slow-growing plant with yellow-green foliage which in autumn assumes a dazzling golden hue, which is lost in full sun. The plant should therefore be planted in a shadier part of the garden.

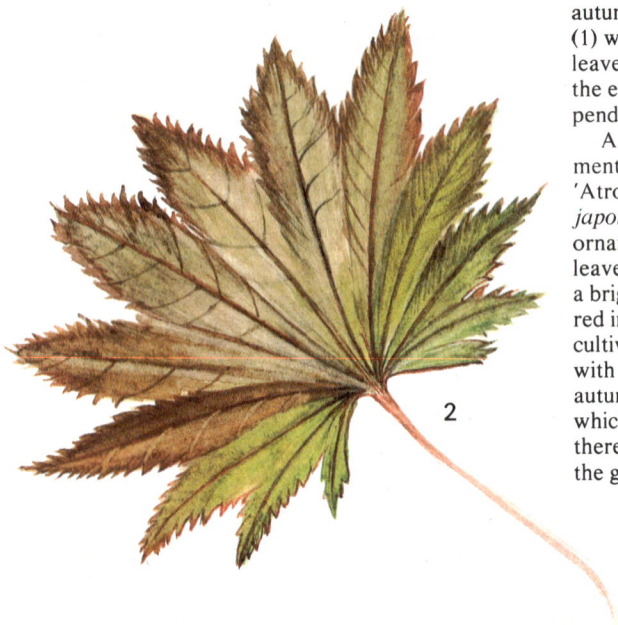

2

1

1

3

21

Milfoil, Yarrow
Achillea serbica

Over one hundred species of Milfoil occur predominantly in the temperate zone of the Northern Hemisphere. The stem is erect and the leaves are alternate, either finely and deeply cut or undivided and form a ground rosette. The flowers are either single and large or tiny and arranged in a large flat inflorescence (corymbous panicle). The fruit is a smooth achene. The low-growing species, such as *A. serbica*, are planted in rock gardens, the taller ones, such as *A. filipendulina*, up to 5 ft (1.5 m) high, with large, flat panicles of tiny yellow florets, can be used as focal points of the edge of the rock garden. Some undemanding species of Milfoil can be used to cover areas unsuitable for other plants.

Achillea millefolium occurs in the wild in Britain and throughout Europe. This botanical species would probably not be used in the rock garden, but some of its cultivars are highly ornamental, such as 'Kelwayi' with red flowers, the red-flowering 'Sammetriese', 2 to 3 ft (60 cm to 1 m) tall, or the pink-flowering 'Cerise Queen', 1½ to 2 ft (45 to 60 cm) tall.

Milfoils require full sun, good drainage and poor, sandy, light soil. They are very undemanding and propagated by division, cuttings or from seed sown in spring.

Achillea serbica (1) is a native of the Balkans. It is covered with grey felt and grows to height of 6 to 8 in (15 to 20 cm), with silvery-grey, narrow serrate leaves. The leafy stem bears one to three flower heads resembling small ox-eye daisies. The outer ray florets are white and tiny and the yellow florets form a disc. The flowering period is from June to July.

Achillea ageratifolia from Macedonia is a similar but later flowering plant. The leaves are also silvery-grey but pinnate and each stem bears only one large flower.

Dry and stony spots in the rock garden are successfully covered with *Achillea chrysocoma* (2), 6 to 8 in (15 to 20 cm) high, with finely cut, white-felted leaves. Creeping shoots grow from small ground rosettes to form new plantlets which send out roots and make the plant spread in greyish carpets. The flowering season is in May and June, sometimes August.

Achillea millefolium 'Kelwayi' (3) has impressive, dazzling red flowers in the late summer, but it is invasive.

3

2

1

23

Spring Adonis
Adonis vernalis

Ranunculaceae

Adonises are annual or perennial plants distributed in Europe and Asia. They have finely-divided leaves and solitary terminal flowers on little-branched stems. Recommended for the rock garden are the species *A. vernalis* and *A. amurensis,* having large yellow flowers.

The Spring Adonis (*Adonis vernalis*) is planted in a sunny position, in loamy, light, calcareous soil. It does poorly in acid soil. It will live long in one spot, under favourable conditions spreading in beautiful and profusely blossoming clumps. Space requirements have to be taken into account when the plant is set out. The stems become elongated after flowering when the plant is at its least attractive.

Propagation is by division of the clumps after flowering or by seed sown as soon as it is ripe. The seedlings grow slowly.

Adonis amurensis is cultivated in a different manner. It requires humus-rich soil, partial shade and a moist site, so it is suitable for wooded parts of the garden. It does not form viable seeds in Britain or central Europe, and so has to be propagated by division.

The Spring Adonis (*Adonis vernalis*) (1) is found on the warm sunny slopes and stony plains of southeastern and central Europe, mainly on loamy acidic soils. It is a protected plant, but it can be easily propagated in the garden. It is 4 in to 1 ft (10 to 30 cm) high and the solitary, dazzlingly yellow, glossy flowers measure up to 2¾ in (7 cm) across. In the flowering period, from April to May, it is a beautiful and eye-catching ornament. The fruit is a beak-shaped, wrinkled achene, attached to a cylindrical receptacle (2).

Adonis amurensis (3) from Manchuria is much rarer. It is similar to the previously mentioned species but the leaves are divided into broader segments and develop fully either with the flowers or, more frequently, after flowering. The yellow flowers are somewhat smaller and the flowering season starts in February or March.

1

3

Candytuft
Aethionema rotundifolium   Cruciferae

Candytufts are annual or perennial plants or sub-shrubs. About 40 species exist distributed mainly in the Near East, although a few species occur in Europe. They have all the features of alpine plants: small, glabrous, grey-green leaves with entire margin, and relatively large, white, pinkish to purple flowers in racemes. The most frequently cultivated are *Aethionema grandiflorum* and *A. rotundifolium,* now bearing a new name of *Eunomia rotundifolia,* but the older name is still commonly used in books on gardening.

Candytufts can be planted both in sunny and shaded situations. They need good soil drainage. Gravel or coarse sand should be added to the soil to make it light and pervious, and seedlings are surrounded by crushed gravel. Candytufts do well in rocky crevices or on screes.

It is best to propagate them from seed, sown under glass immediately after ripening or early in spring. Some species can be propagated by division, others by cuttings which are inserted in sifted sandy soil in a heated propagator from June to August.

Aethionema rotundifolium (1), which is only 1 to 2 in (2½ to 5 cm) high, comes from the Caucasus. It is a low-growing, mat-forming species suitable even for miniature rock gardens or troughs. The short leafy stems are terminated by clusters of tiny pink flowers. The combination of grey-green foliage and pink flowers is very impressive at the time of flowering in April and May. The fruits are siliquas with a winged margin (2).

Aethionema grandiflorum (3) is much taller — 8 in to 1 ft (20 to 30 cm) — and bears racemes of large pink flowers which appear from May to July.

The hybrid called Lebanon Candytuft or Store Cress (*Aethionema warleyense*) is often encountered in rock gardens. It is similar to the species *A. grandiflorum* which is probably one of its parents, but it has broader leaves and larger flowers. The flowers in the cultivar 'Warley Rose' are pink, and in 'Warley Ruber' they are dark red.

2

3

Flowering Onion
Allium oreophilum
Liliaceae

The genus *Allium* comprises some 280 species distributed almost all over the world. These bulbous plants are found both in dry, sunny places and in moist, humus-rich forests, and from lowland mountainous areas. They show a variety of different features, from low-growing species to those reaching 5 ft (1½ m) in height, such as *A. giganteum*, a native of the Himalayas, which is impressive as a solitary plant in the vicinity of the rock garden. The genus *Allium* also covers a broad spectrum of colours: violet, yellow (*A. moly*) pink (*A. oreophilum*), blue or white. The fruits are capsules which are often used in dried flower arrangements.

Cultivation is straightforward. The plants are set out in sandy-loamy soil in a well-drained sunny position. The bulbs are planted in September and October. Small bulbs are planted 2 to 3 in (5 to 8 cm) deep, large bulbs, like *Allium giganteum*, are planted 8 in (20 cm) deep. The plants can remain in the same spot for several years. They should always be transplanted after the leaves have turned yellow.

Propagation is also possible from bulbils which are formed on the flowerheads. Propagation by seed takes a long time.

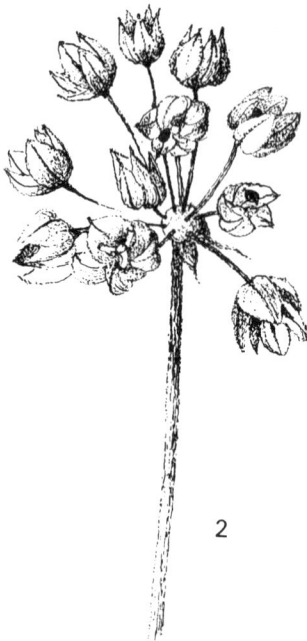

2

The low-growing species include *Allium oreophilum* and *A. ostrowskianum* (1) from Turkestan. The latter is an undemanding plant which brightens the rock garden in the flowering period with a profusion of relatively large pink flowers. The heads (2) are used for dried flower arrangements.

The Golden Garlic (*A. moly*) (3) from southern Europe is a popular species. It has a smallish white bulb (4) from which grow grey-green leaves, about ½ in (1 cm) wide, and the flower-bearing stalk, which reaches a height of 8 in to 1 ft (20 to 30 cm). The stalk is terminated by a rich umbel of yellow flowers appearing from May to July. *Allium moly* can be planted either in the sun or in semi-shade, for instance under trees with a light canopy. It spreads readily, but one of its disadvantages, which it shares with other species of the genus, is the yellowing of the leaves during and after the flowering period.

Mountain Alyssum
Alyssum montanum — Cruciferae

Out of many species of *Alyssum,* only some of those with European origin are suited to rock-garden cultivation. They differ in their habits; some form low cushions, such as *A. montanum* or *A. moellendorfianum;* others develop into open prickly shrubs with white or pink flowers, like *A. spinosum* (*Ptilotrichum spinosum*). The most frequently cultivated is *A. saxatile* and its cultivars, e.g. the double-flowered 'Plenum' or 'Citrinum' with lemon-yellow flowers or 'Variegatum' with yellow-white streaked leaves. The cultivar 'Compactum', only 4½ to 6 in (12 to 15 cm) high, is suitable for smaller rock gardens.

Alyssums grow on dry rocks exposed to the sun and occur both in the lowlands and on mountainsides. They are undemanding and hardy plants. To ensure a wealth of flowers, plant in well-drained sandy to stony soil in full sun. They flourish in rocky fissures or on dry walls, where they spread readily to produce beautiful garlands of yellow flowers. Rich loamy soil makes them grow too fast and they die soon. Although in the wild their occurrence is restricted mainly to limestone rocks, in the rock garden they will survive on acid soil. Cut the plants back by a third as soon as the flowering period is over to keep the growth compact.

The easiest method of propagation is by seed which is formed in great quantity. They tend to sow themselves freely and the seedlings bear flowers the following year. The garden varieties are propagated by cuttings taken after flowering has finished.

The Mountain Alyssum (*Alyssum montanum*) (1) is a profusely flowering plant, about 2 to 4 in (5 to 10 cm) tall, grey-green all over. The trailing leafy stem turns woody at the base and has an upturned end. The small evergreen leaves are covered with stellate hairs and the leafy stems bear racemes of yellow flowers. The fruits are siliquas each containing two seeds. The Mountain Alyssum flowers from April to June, often with a second flush. The fruit-bearing period is in late summer.

Alyssum saxatile (2) spreads to form large clumps, 12 to 18 in (30 to 45 cm) tall. From April to June, at the height of the flowering period, it is one of the most beautiful plants in the rock garden and in the wild. The fruit is a rounded siliqua containing one or two seeds (3, 4).

1

2

3

4

Anacyclus depressus

There are several species of the genus *Anacyclus,* distributed mainly in the Mediterranean, but only *A. depressus* is cultivated in rock gardens so far. It is native to northern Africa where it grows in the mountain regions of Morocco.

Successful cultivation of this attractive plant requires a position in full sun with sandy soil supplemented with limestone gravel to make it really well drained. The best sites are scree slopes, crevices between rocks and on dry walls. If the plant withers before flowering, it does not mean it has died. This is probably caused by excessive moisture, and can be remedied by keeping the plant in a dry situation. It should then grow again the following year; good drainage is a prerequisite of successful cultivation. This plant takes some time to get used to a new site so if it is situated in a rocky fissure, it must be given ample space to spread its branches in a circle, otherwise it would lose its interesting shape. It should be protected from damp in winter.

Anacyclus depressus is propagated from the seed, sown immediately after ripening. It is left in a cold frame over winter, and the seedlings are planted out in the open in early spring. In favourable conditions the plants sometimes sow themselves.

Anacyclus depressus (1) is an interesting rock garden plant. It looks very decorative in suitable sites, because its trailing, leafy stems spread out in circles. The dark green leaves are finely cut, and the plant is only 2 to 4 in (5 to 10 cm) high. The ends of the stems are erect and terminated by flowerheads resembling small daisies. The outer ray florets are carmine-pink (2) on the outside, and the buds are therefore pink. The white outside florets and the yellow disc appear only when the flower opens. The flowering period is from May to July.

The flowers are arranged in the type of inflorescence called a capitulum, which is typical of the whole family Compositae. The capitulum is composed of a large number of small florets which together imitate the structure of a single flower (3). The central florets are regular, the outer ones are usually ray-shaped but are not necessarily present.

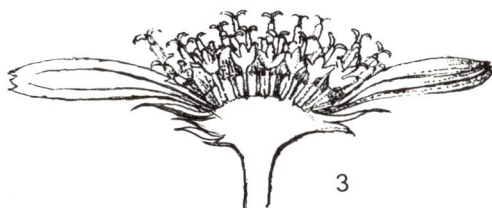

Androsace ciliata

Androsaces are low-growing, usually alpine plants. Their leaf rosettes form thick cushions or mats. They cover a large number of species. Some are easy to cultivate, others are more difficult to grow and some require an alpine house. The genus is divided into four groups: *Pseudoprimula, Chamaejasme, Aretia* and *Andrapsis*. The *Pseudoprimula* group comprises predominantly the Asiatic species. These need light shade to full shade conditions, and their cultivation is demanding. The *Chamaejasme* group includes mountain species which are most frequently cultivated. They require partial shade and normal garden soil. They spread readily to form tidy mats. The *Aretia* group contains the lowest-growing plants from high altitudes, forming compact mats. Unfortunately they are delicate and difficult to keep in the rock garden, or they produce few flowers (except *Androsace ciliata*). They need sandy or stony soil with good drainage and a situation turned away from the sun. They succeed best in stone crevices. The *Andrapsis* group covers annual species which are mostly self-sown. Androsaces are easily propagated by division of the leaf rosettes, by cuttings or from the seed sown after ripening.

4

Androsace ciliata (1) is one of the few members of the *Aretia* group which can be successfully cultivated in the rock garden. It is native to the Pyrenees where it grows in rocky fissures on limestone, at heights of up to 13,150 ft (4,000 m). It flowers from March to May.

One of the less demanding species is *Androsace lactea* (2) from the *Chamaejasme* group. It occurs at the sub-alpine or alpine levels of European mountain ranges, on limestone rocks. It has a wealth of flowers from May to June. The fruit is a capsule (3).

Androsace primuloides (4) from the *Chamaejasme* group is indigenous to the Himalayas. The leaf rosette sends out many offshoots terminated by other rosettes which take root and spread to

cover large areas. The same group
includes the successfully growing
A. sempervivoides (5) which flowers from
May to June, and *A. mucronifolia* (6),
producing pure pink blooms in April and
May and offshoots later on (7).

3

1

6

2

5

Anemone
Anemone apennina

Anemones are found mainly in the Northern Hemisphere. Some species are tuberous (e. g. *Anemone apennina, A. blanda*), others have a thin rhizome (e. g. *A. nemorosa, A. ranunculoides*) or fascicular roots (e. g. *A. narcissiflora*). They comprise low-growing plants 4 to 6 in (10 to 15 cm) in height and spread, and those attaining a height of 3 ft (1 m) or more. Some bloom early, others flower in autumn. They also differ in their ecological requirements. Some species have been improved by cultivation, and many cultivars are available, particularly in the species *A. apennina, A. nemorosa*, or in the tall Japanese Anemone *(A. japonica)*, flowering in autumn.

Anemones are easily propagated from the seed. The seeds germinate well but have to be sown immediately after ripening. The ovaries ripen into achenes which differ according to species; they can be glabrous, hairy or shrivelled. The tuberous species can be propagated by separating a part of the tuber in July.

The beautiful *Anemone apennina* (1) is frequently cultivated. The dark brown, irregular tubers resemble small lumps of earth. The large flower is composed of eight to fourteen narrow blue petals. Cultivars of various colours are grown in specialist nurseries. This delightful plant flowers early in spring and attracts attention by its fragile beauty. It is found in southern Europe in humus-rich deciduous woodland. The tubers should therefore be planted in loamy soil, some 2¼ in (6 cm) deep, in light shade. The plants do well in wooded parts of the garden under deciduous shrubs, where they have sufficient humus and ample sunshine in spring. A thick growth is achieved by avoiding unnecessary transfers. Of similar appearance is *A. blanda,* a native of Greece and Asia Minor.

Anemone narcissiflora (2) has a totally different habit. It is rather tall, but in a suitable spot, for instance in an alpine meadow at the side of a rock garden, it can be highly decorative. Its home is in the mountains of central Europe, northern Asia and North America, where it usually grows on limestone. It is planted in moist but well-drained loamy soil with extra gravel incorporated, in a place protected from the sun. It can be cultivated in an acid soil.

The well-known spring plants native to European deciduous woodland include *Anemone nemorosa* (3). This prefers the wooded part of the rock garden. It has also a double-flowered form, *A. n. plena.*

1

2

3

Mountain Everlasting, Mountain Cat's-ear
Antennaria dioica
Compositae

Antennarias are undemanding carpeting plants. They have entire, undivided leaves forming ground rosettes from which grow leafy stems and numerous creeping, leafy offshoots. The entire plant is covered with silky hairs. The stem is erect and bears linear leaves. It is terminated by pink or white flowerheads. As the Latin name implies, *A. dioica* is a dioecious plant, which means that an individual bears either only female flowers or has male and hermaphrodite flowers (3). The fruit is an achene.

Antennarias are very tolerant plants. They are grown in dry, sunny situations and planted in poor, sandy, acid soil. They can be used in places where not even grass would grow. In rich loamy soil in semi-shade they lose their handsome compact growth and the stems become too tall.

They spread freely owing to the stoloniferous roots which most species have and can be easily propagated by division, best in spring or autumn. If given sufficient space, they soon form tidy silvery carpets.

The Mountain Everlasting, *Antennaria dioica* (1) is common in dry situations, pastures, sunny slopes or the alpine meadows of central Europe. The flowering stems are 2 to 6 in (5 to 15 cm) high, and the leaf rosettes form low and dense silvery mats, particularly in sunny conditions. There are a number of cultivars which are grown in gardens: 'Tomentosa' has hairy, white felt-like leaves, 'Rubra' has carmine-pink flowers (2) and 'Minima', which is only 2 to 3 in (5 to 8 cm) tall, is particularly suited to small rock gardens.

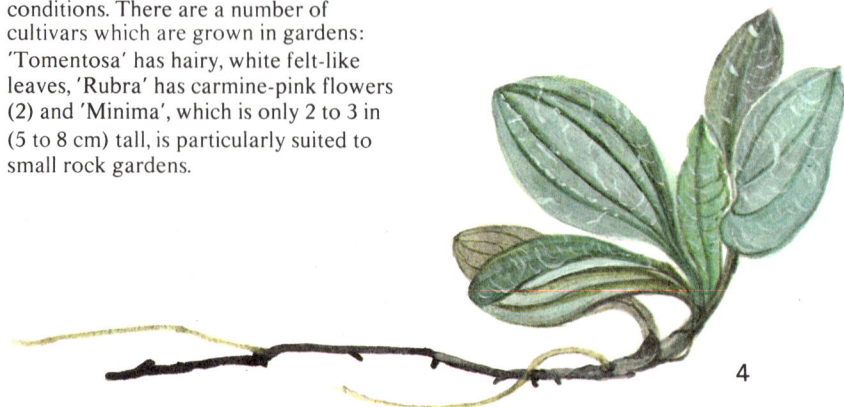

4

A more robust species is *Antennaria plantaginifolia* (4), originating in North America, with broadly oval, felted leaves, similar in shape to the leaves of Ribgrass. The leafy stems are often up to 1½ ft (45 cm) tall, and for this reason the plant should be chosen for larger rock gardens. The inflorescence is larger than that of *A. dioica,* and flowering is from April to June. It is also undemanding and will soon cover a large space. It can be situated in places where other alpine plants will not grow.

2

1

3

Columbine
Aquilegia discolor

Ranunculaceae

Columbines are distributed over the northern temperate zone. They are delicate plants with ornamental flowers of various colours. The leaves have three segments, each bi- or tri-ternate, held on long petioles. The interesting flower has petaloid sepals of various colours and five concave petals which elongate into spurs. The length of the spur varies between species and it is hooked in various ways; in some cases the spur is absent. Columbines are classified according to the length and shape of their spurs.

Columbines are very easy to grow. They thrive in ordinary garden soil, both in a sunny place and in semi-shade. They are propagated from the seed and often sow themselves. They often crossbreed themselves, so if a pure species or a specific colour is to be preserved, the plant must be protected from pollination by another species or alternatively propagated by cuttings.

There are many cultivars with flowers of different colours and shapes. Tall plants are better suited for bedding schemes rather than for rockeries where they could produce a disturbing, unnatural effect.

The large number of columbines include some low-growing species suitable for small rockeries. One such is *Aquilegia discolor* (1), a native of the Pyrenees, only 4 to 6 in (10 to 15 cm) high. The flowers on long stalks have blue petals with a spur and a cream-coloured calyx. This species flowers in May and June, sometimes even in July. The fruit is a follicle. *Aquilegia akitensis* is of similar appearance.

Aquilegia ecalcarata (2) has flowers without spurs, and it is therefore classified by some experts in an independent genus when it is known as *Semiaquilegia ecalcarata*. It is 6 to 8 in (15 to 20 cm) tall, the leaves are divided into tiny leaflets, and the mauve flowers are smaller and without spurs. It flowers relatively late, from June to August. It is native to western China and Japan.

A highly ornamental, low-growing columbine from the southern Alps, *Aquilegia bertolonii* (3), has large blue flowers with short hooked spurs and grey-green leaves. The flowers appear in April and May, sometimes even in June.

2

3

1

Rock Cress
Arabis albida Cruciferae

The genus *Arabis* comprises about 100 species found at all altitudes from the lowlands to the mountains. The leaves have different shapes and form rosettes. Some species spread quickly because of their numerous offshoots and create low carpets, e. g. the undemanding *A. procurrens* with tiny green leaves. The flowers are composed of four petals and grow in a raceme, inflorescence typical of the Cruciferae family.

These plants have been cultivated for a long time. The most frequently encountered include the Rock Cress, *Arabis albida* (also known as *A. caucasica*). There are a number of cultivars, including the double-flowered form 'Plena', 'Variegata' with white-streaked leaves and 'Nana', a dwarf form, which are now more often seen in cultivation than the species.

Most species flourish in ordinary garden soil, in a sunny position or in light shade. The plants exposed to the sun are more compact and produce better flowers. They spread quickly and will soon cover a large space. They are particularly suited for planting dry stone walls.

Propagation presents no problems. The best method is division after flowering. Alternatively seed can be sown or cuttings taken in autumn or early spring. Cultivars can only be propagated by division or by taking cuttings.

The Rock Cress (1) is a well-known and undemanding rock garden plant. A 6 to 8 in (15 to 20 cm) high, leafy stalk with white flowers in a long raceme grows from an attractive rosette of greyish-green, irregularly-toothed leaves. A profusion of flowers is produced in April and May. The fruit is a narrow, long siliqua (4).

The hybrid *Arabis arendsii* is very similar and quickly spreads by numerous creeping offshoots. It has several attractive cultivars; 'Rosabella' has beautiful pink flowers (2), 'Coccinea' and 'Atrorosea' have large, rich reddish-pink blooms.

The smaller *Arabis vochinensis* (3) forms a very low, ornamental mat. It has an interesting variegated cultivar with white-streaked leaves. Masses of violet buds appear in spring in the middle of the small rosettes of white-rimmed leaves.

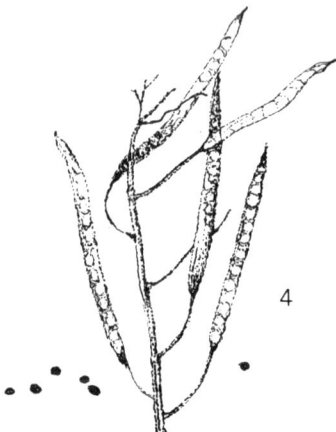

The latter are sessile at first, and later the flowers open on a stalk which is 2 to 4 in (5 to 10 cm) high. As this happens the violet colour disappears to leave the flower pure white.

1

2

3

Sandwort
Arenaria tetraquetra   Caryophyllaceae

Sandworts exist in about 160 species. There are both annual and perennial plants found almost all over the world. They have opposite leaves and flowers with five petals, single or in small clusters. The fruit is a capsule containing black seeds.

They require well-drained, gritty or sandy loam. They do well on limy or acid rocks, although in the wild they prefer limestone. Some species like full sun, others prefer less exposed sites or light shade. They form low mats or smallish, dense cushions.

Propagation is by seed or division before or after flowering. From June to August they can be propagated by cuttings.

Arenaria tetraquetra (1) is a small-sized 1 in (2½ cm) high plant from the Pyrenees and Spain. Tiny dense leaves grow on short stems giving these latter the appearance of being four-sided. Two to three white terminal flowers with five petals appear from May to July. The plant forms firm cushions and it is highly ornamental even outside the flowering period. It succeeds best in rocky crevices and is suitable for small rockeries or trough gardens.

Arenaria purpurascens (3) from the Pyrenees is more robust. The leafy, trailing stems spread in tidy, low mats. The reddish stems are terminated by pale pink, star-shaped flowers with five pointed petals. They flower in June and July, sometimes even in August. The fruit is a capsule (4). This plant does well in the sun but can tolerate light shade.

The Balearic Islands and Corsica are the homes of one of the lowest-growing species, *Arenaria balearica* (2). This has fast-growing, densely leaf-covered stems which literally smother the ground and stones, so they look as if they were covered with moss. From May to August, single flowers with white petals arranged in a star pattern appear on 1 to 1½ in (2.5 to 4 cm) tall stalks. The plant is set out in partial or full shade in a moist situation. It often disappears from its original site, but as a rule reappears somewhere else.

2

3

Thrift
Armeria caespitosa   Plumbaginaceae

All species of the genus *Armeria* form tufts of linear, rather spiky leaves growing from a thick rootstock. The flowers are clustered at the end of a single, unbranched stalk in globose umbels. The parts of the bracts are turned downwards and form a tube embracing the stem. The corolla is composed of five petals which are fused at the base.

Thrifts are easy to cultivate. Most are hardy but a few including *Armeria caespitosa* are rather tender. All species require full sun and well-drained sandy or stony, preferably poor soil. Good drainage and acid soil are basic prerequisites of successful cultivation, because thrifts do not tolerate lime. *A. caespitosa* prefers a situation away from the sun. The winter damp is particularly harmful, and the plants should be covered with glass or other material, particularly in places prone to rainy winters.

Thrifts are propagated by division after flowering, by taking cuttings or from seed.

Armeria caespitosa (1) is a low-growing alpine plant from Spain and Portugal, where it is found in the mountains up to a height of 9,850 ft (3,000 m). It makes close-set cushions, only about 2 in (5 to 6 cm) high in the flowering period. The leaves form a compact ground rosette spreading into large cushions. In old age they tend to disintegrate from the centre, where an empty spot appears. The pink flowers open from April to May in great profusion, often entirely covering the green leaf rosettes.

One of the commonly cultivated higher species is the Sea Pink, *Armeria maritima* (2). It blooms in May and June and often produces flowers in autumn as well. It flourishes in rockeries without special care. It is native to north-western Europe and North America. It occurs in dry, sunny places in the wild. Several cultivars are grown: 'Alba' with white flowers (3), 'Rosea' with carmine-pink flowers, 'Laucheana' with carmine-red blooms, and others.

Armeria welwitschii (4), a native of Spain, can be planted in a large rockery. So far it has been scarcely encountered in cultivation, perhaps because of its robust growth in comparison with the previous species. Its leaves are up to ¼ in (5 mm) wide and 3 to 4 in (8 to 10 cm) long. The stems are about 1 ft (30 cm) tall. The umbels of pure pink flowers are up to 1 in (2.5 cm) wide. The flowering season lasts all summer, until the first frost.

4

2

3

Woodruff
Asperula nitida

Rubiaceae

The genus *Asperula* contains some 90 species distributed throughout Europe, particularly in the Mediterranean, and in Asia. Some species occur in Australia. They are annual to perennial plants with leaves arranged apparently in whorls. The stems are erect or trailing, and the flowers are in clusters at the ends of branches. The corolla is funnel-shaped, sometimes quite prominently, with four points. The fruit is a diachene.

Asperula odorata, reaching a height of up to 2½ ft (45 cm), is a denizen of European woodlands rich in humus. The pale green, lanceolate leaves turn black when dry and give off a smell of coumarin. From May to June, the Woodruff produces tiny white flowers. In the garden, it is situated in the wooded section.

The alpine species are best suited for rockeries (e. g. the most often cultivated *Asperula nitida*). These low-growing plants, mostly with trailing stems, form more or less dense cushions or low carpets. All of them are beautiful, long-flowering rockery plants. They are set out in sunny positions in stony, humus-rich soil with good drainage. Some species are highly sensitive to damp and must be protected from it, particularly in winter.

Propagation is by division in early spring, or by seed, although the cultivated species usually do not form seeds.

Asperula nitida (1) comes from northern Greece. It forms dense, dark green mats, only 1 to 2 in (2½ to 5 cm) high. The tips of the narrow leaves are bristly. In June and July the trailing stems are terminated by rather rich inflorescences of pale pink flowers.

The beautiful but demanding and delicate *Asperula arcadiensis* (2) is also a native of the Greek mountains. It forms grey and sparse cushions, about 4 in (10 cm) high. The leaves are fine, linear, with erect hairs. The trailing, leafy stems are terminated by four to ten flowers. The dainty, relatively large pink blooms have a conspicuously long funnel. The plant must be situated in a spot which is not exposed to the sun. It thrives in rocky crevices of a limestone rockery. It is very particular over the amount of moisture it receives.

Asperula hirta from the Pyrenees forms dense but loose cushions, 4 to 6 in (10 to 15 cm) high. It has rich green foliage and pinkish-white flowers which appear from May to June or longer, and often again in autumn. A white form — 'Alba' (3) — is also cultivated.

2

3

Maidenhair Spleenwort
Asplenium trichomanes
Aspleniaceae

Shady situations in the rock garden are suitable for ferns. Almost all species of *Asplenium* can be accommodated even in small rockeries. They are low-growing ferns, with fronds anything from 2 in to 2 ft (5 cm to 60 cm) long.

Ferns are propagated by spores distributed by the wind. The spores are stored in spore receptacles known as sori which vary in shape according to species and are situated on the underside of the fronds (4). The young fronds of the emerging fern are spirally rolled up; this is typical of all young ferns.

Unlike most other ferns, the Maidenhair Spleenwort, *Asplenium trichomanes,* does not tolerate a permanently moist position in winter, and should be situated in a shaded rocky crevice in sandy-loamy soil. It is propagated from spores or by division of larger clumps in spring.

Asplenium trichomanes (1) has a stout rootstock from which grow evergreen pinnate fronds, 2 to 8 in (5 to 20 cm) long. The petiole is dark brown, the leaves are ovoid, toothed, dark green. The elongated linear sori are on the back of the fronds.

The Maidenhair Spleenwort is found in Europe, Asia and America, on rocks, walls and in stony woodland. Closely resembling this species is *A. viride.* It differs in longer leaves and green petioles. It grows on limestone rocks.

Another small fern, only 4 to 6 in (10 to 15 cm) high, is *Asplenium septentrionale* (2). The fronds are simple or divided into narrow, fork-like segments. Almost the entire underside is covered with sori. The plant can be grown in either a sunny or shaded position, but it will not tolerate lime in the soil.

Asplenium ruta-muraria (3) is a small fern with fronds 2 to 4 in (5 to 10 cm) long. Bi- or tri-pinnate evergreen fronds grow from the crown. This fern requires a well-drained position and in the wild it often grows in cracked walls, always on a limy base, in both sunny or shaded spots.

4

2

3

1

Alpine Aster
Aster alpinus   Compositae

This extensive genus embraces many species and cultivars of varying shapes and colours. Asters are perennial or annual. They are usually rather tall, and some can be used as solitary plants in the vicinity of the rock garden. Many low asters are available in the wide selection of species.

Asters are undemanding and hardy plants for rockeries. They do well in ordinary garden soil, both in the sun and in the shade. The plants cultivated in the sun and in poor soil tend to be low-growing and therefore more suitable for rock gardens than the plants flourishing in loamy soil and semi-shade.

Propagation is by division and very easy. Botanical species can be propagated by seed.

Aster alpinus (1) is the best-known species, probably present in most rock gardens. The grey-green, hairy leaves form tidy basal rosettes and there is a single, large flower head on a stem, 4 to 8 in (10 to 20 cm) tall and sparsely covered with leaves. The flowers appear in May and June. In the wild the Alpine Aster grows in the mountains of Europe, Asia and America, occurring on stony and grassy slopes exposed to the sun. There are many cultivars differing chiefly in the colour of the flowers: 'Albus' with white flowers, 'Rex' with pale blue flowers, the pink 'Roseus Superbus' (2), and many others.

One of the smallest species is *Aster andersonii* (3) from North America; it is only 2 to 3½ in (5 to 7 cm) high. The alternate, bright green leaves grow on prostrate stems. The flowering period is in June. It is an undemanding species and often becomes invasive, so it needs plenty of space and will soon make a neat, rich green carpet, highly ornamental in the flowering season.

Of interest, too, is the North American *Aster dumosus* (4). It forms a compact, semi-globose shrub, which in autumn becomes virtually clothed in blossoms. It has many cultivars of various colours and sizes ranging from 6 to 20 in (15 to 50 cm). The lowest-growing types are naturally best for the rock garden. They produce a profusion of flowers from September to October, at the time when blossoms become rare in the garden.

Barberry
Berberis candidula

The genus *Berberis* comprises over 500 species distributed in Europe, Asia, North America and Africa. The small or large shrubs are either evergreen or deciduous. The leaves are modified into spines (1 — 3), and in their axils grow short branches with clustered leaves. The yellow or orange blossoms are single, in clusters or pendent racemes. The fruit is an oval, red, blue to reddish-blue berry. Many cultivars have originated from easy crossing of species. These undemanding woody plants do well in the sun and semi-shade, in ordinary garden soil. They can be slightly damaged by frost in severe winters, but they recover in spring.

Barberries are easily propagated by seed sown in autumn or early spring after stratification. Cultivars have to be propagated by cuttings which should take root readily. Deciduous species are propagated by half-ripe cuttings in June and July; for evergreen species take hardwood cuttings in October and November.

The small evergreen shrub *Berberis candidula* (1) attains a height of 1½ ft (45 cm) and a width of about 2 ft (60 cm). The leaves are single, small, glossy and rich green above and silvery-white below, roughly toothed and spiny on the margins. The single, bright yellow blossoms appear in May and June. They ripen into blue berries.

The ornamental deciduous *Berberis thunbergii,* 3 to 5 ft (1 to 1.5 m) high, has small, single, highly variable leaves with entire margin, assuming rich red tints in autumn. The yellow flowers appear in May. The fruits are bright red, oval berries (3). 'Atropurpurea' (2) is a frequently planted cultivar. The young leaves are a bronzy red, later turning

4

1

darker, and in autumn they become carmine-red. This shrub, ornamental both in terms of shape and coloration, can be used as a solitary plant or in hedges, because it tolerates cutting. Much better suited to the rock garden than either the species or 'Atropurpurea' is the cultivar 'Atropurpurea Nana' which is only 1 ft (30 cm) high.

Evergreen barberries include *Berberis verruculosa* (4) originating in China. In May and June it produces single yellow flowers. The fruits are purplish violet at first, later becoming black.

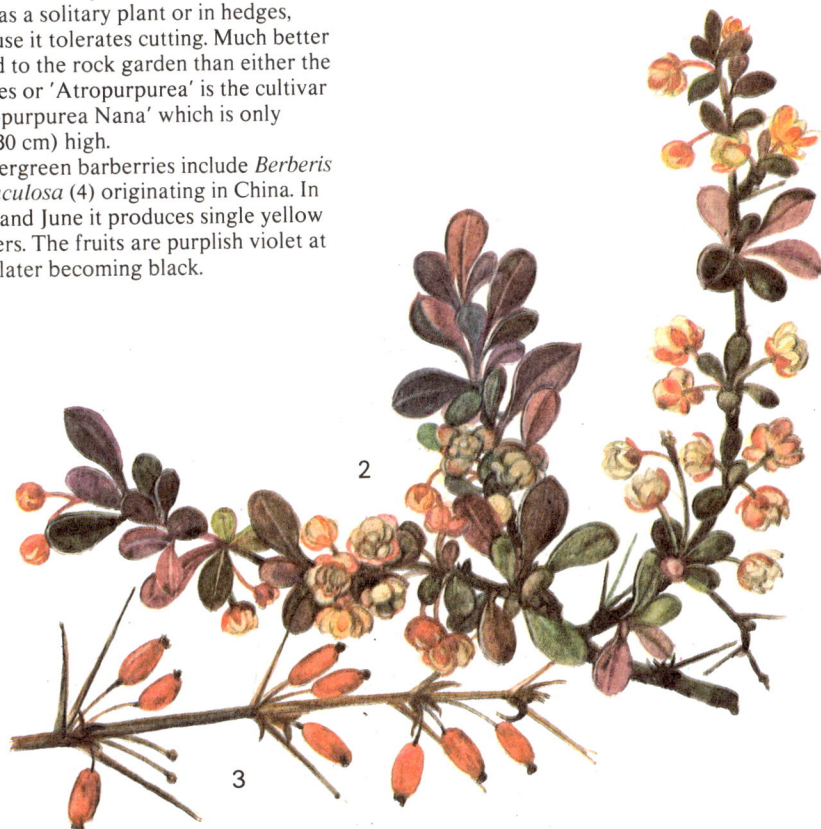

2

3

Slipper Flower
Calceolaria biflora

Although the genus *Calceolaria* comprises about 300 species, only a few of them are cultivated in rock gardens. Their principal area of distribution covers the mountain regions of South America and New Zealand. They include beautiful, low-growing plants such as *C. darwinii*, *C. tenella*, *C. umbellata* and others, which are seldom encountered in cultivation. The rarely cultivated *C. forthergillii*, a native of Patagonia and the Falkland Islands, could survive outside under favourable conditions. It is 4 in (10 cm) high, and has hairy leaves and single yellow flowers with red dots. It requires a shaded situation with good drainage. Slipper flowers also include *C. mexicana* from the mountain ranges of Mexico. It has small pale yellow flowers and undemanding habits. *C. biflora* and *C. polyrrhiza* are the most frequently and easily cultivated species.

Slipper flowers have an interesting two-lipped blossom. The upper lip is small, the lower one is markedly larger and resembles a slipper. In the rock garden, the plants should be planted in semi-shade or shade, in a sheltered position. They need well-drained acid soil, rich in humus but also gritty. They should be covered in winter. They are easily propagated from the seed, sometimes sowing themselves and appearing in distant places where the wind carries the light seeds. They can also be propagated by division, best in March and April.

The delicate *Calceolaria biflora* (1) with a yellow 'slipper' on a thin stalk is native to Chile and Argentina. It has broad, oval to rounded leaves with entire margins arranged in an appressed ground rosette. The foliage is similar to the Ribgrass (*Plantago*), and it is consequently sometimes called *C. plantaginea*. From the centre of the rosette grow several stems, 4 to 6 in (10 to 15 cm) high, with one or two flowers, about 1/2 in (1 cm) wide, yellow in colour and speckled with red. It flowers in May and June, sometimes in July. The fruit is a capsule

(3) with two sections containing a large number of fine seeds.

Patagonia is the homeland of *Calceolaria polyrrhiza* (2) which has lanceolate leaves up to 10 cm long, arranged in a ground rosette. The single yellow flowers have a prominent lower lip speckled with purplish red. The flowering period is in June and July. In suitable places, the plant spreads freely by creeping offshoots. The cultivar 'John Innes' has larger flowers but it is delicate and has to be well covered in winter.

3

1

2

Bellflower
Campanula cochleariifolia   Campanulaceae

Bellflowers are a must for every rock garden. They come in different shapes and sizes, and there is a wide choice of low-growing species. The genus *Campanula* includes some 250 species distributed throughout the Northern Hemisphere. They are mostly perennial plants with leaves that vary in shape. The stem is leafy and the flowers are bell-shaped, either single or arranged in different types of inflorescence. The fruit is a capsule containing numerous seeds.

Bellflowers are easily propagated by seed, division or cuttings. Slugs and snails can be a problem so take measures against these pests by scattering slug bait around the plants.

Campanula cochleariifolia (1) is one of the more vigorous bellflowers producing a profusion of long-lived flowers. It is small, 2 to 4 in (5 to 10 cm) high, with single or double nodding flowers. The pale blue corolla is just over ½ in (1 cm) long and has short points. It flowers from June to August. In the wild it grows on the limestone screes and rocks on the mountains of Europe. In the rock garden, it sometimes spreads too fast into bright green carpets, attractive mainly when in blossom. It spreads by thin runners which easily grow under stones, and so it should be planted only in a situation where it cannot swamp other species. There are numerous cultivars which vary in the colour of their flowers, although the majority are white (2). The blooms are large and semi-double.

Beautiful large flowers are produced by *Campanula tridentata* (3). It is 4 to 6 in (10 to 15 cm) high and has narrow leaves with entire margins but with three

4

slight teeth on the tips. The leaves form
a dense ground rosette from which grow
stems bearing several single flowers. The
corolla is bright blue with a white centre.
The flowering period is in April and May;
sometimes flowers are produced at the
end of summer. The soil should be rich in
humus and the planting position away
from the sun.

Campanula elatines (4) has an entirely
different flower shape and its fragile
stems trail. It forms cushions dotted with
a wealth of flowers opening into stars. It
flourishes in rocky fissures in semi-shaded
positions.

Sedge
Carex firma

Sedges resemble grasses in appearance. The genus *Carex* contains a large number of species which vary in size, appearance and in their ecological requirements. In the wild they are to be found on high mountains, in arctic regions, as well as in peat bogs, wet acid meadows, marshes and on sandy sites. A particular sedge can therefore be found for any part of the garden. Some form small firm cushions, others make large tufts or spread into green carpets. The flowers are monoecious or dioecious, and composed of one or several spikelets. They can be bisexual or unisexual. The fruit is an achene enclosed in a kind of follicle. Sedges are ornamental when flowering with large showy anthers hanging on thin filaments. Propagation is by division, best carried out in spring.

Carex firma forms firm, dense cushions. The stalks are 2 to 4 in (5 to 10 cm) high and terminated by a club-shaped spikelet of male flowers; underneath this are two or three petiolate female spikelets. This species grows naturally in the subalpine regions of European mountains, where it is usually found on limestone. It should be situated in a sunny spot of a limestone rockery, preferably in a rocky fissure and in humusy soil. The cultivar 'Variegata' (1) with streaked leaves is highly ornamental and more frequently cultivated.

Carex montana (2) forms dense clumps with narrow, straight leaves, only $^1/_8$ in (2 mm) wide. The leaves are at first shorter than the stems with two to four spikelets, but they outgrow them later. The terminal spikelet is male, the others are female. The flowering period is in April and May. The plants need humus-rich soil and a preferably sunny position so its growth will remain low although it spreads quickly.

Carex ornithopoda is native to Britain and the warm regions of central Europe. It occurs in light pine woodland on a limestone bedrock. The cultivar 'Variegata' has leaves with cream bands (3).

4

Carex grayi (4) is noted for its interesting fruit. It comes from North America, it is 20 to 28 in (50 to 70 cm) high and can be effectively used at the border of a rockery pool. The ornamental fruits are used in dried flower arrangements.

1

3

2

Mouse-eared Chickweed, Snow-in-summer
Cerastium tomentosum

Caryophyllaceae

Although the genus *Cerastium* comprises over 100 species, it does not offer many suitable for the rock garden. The plants are not very ornamental. They have opposite leaves with entire margins, more or less hairy. The small white flowers have petals notched in front. The fruit is a cylindrical capsule (4). Two most frequently encountered species are *C. tomentosum* and *C. biebersteinii*; both spread readily and soon cover large areas. They produce a mass of large white flowers in May and June, but even outside the flowering period they are decorative thanks to their silvery-grey foliage. The tiny leaves are narrow and densely covered with hairs on both sides.

They succeed in sunny, dry sites, in poor soil. Both species are suitable for planting on dry walls and will grow in poor, stony situations where they can serve as substitutes for a lawn. Cerastiums are propagated by seed sown at the end of winter or in early spring. They can also be propagated by divison, or by cuttings taken in the autumn.

Cerastium tomentosum (1) is 8 to 14 in (20 to 35 cm) tall and comes from Italy. The most frequently cultivated variety is the small var. *columnae,* only 4 to 6 in (10 to 15 cm) high. This species does not spread too freely and can be recommended for smaller rockeries. It has to be cut back heavily in spring to maintain a nice compact shape.

Of similar but more robust appearance is *Cerastium biebersteinii* (2), a native of the Ukraine and Crimea. It spreads fast and its thin creeping stems grow even under large stones. It takes root readily so if you want to remove it altogether, all offshoots have to be carefully dug out. It is not advisable for small rockeries.

Cerastium alpinum (3), the Alpine Mouse-eared Chickweed, is totally different. It is 2 to 4 in (5 to 10 cm) high and covered in woolly hairs. The stem is terminated by large, white single flowers appearing in May and June. This species is found in screes and on rocks in the Pyrenees, Alps, Carpathians, in the Balkans and Altai, but also in the arctic zone of North America and Scandinavia. In rockeries, it needs good drainage and succeeds in rocky crevices in a sunny position. A quantity of moss peat should be added to stony soil to keep the roots in a moist environment. *C. alpinum* is a fastidious species requiring a lot of care.

Hinoki Cypress
Chamaecyparis obtusa
Cupressaceae

Cypresses are native to North America, Japan and Taiwan. They are tall trees, but a series of dwarf cultivars have been developed, and these are suitable even for small rock gardens. They are comparatively undemanding woody plants, but some are not completely hardy. Two of the more vigorous species are *Chamaecyparis nootkatensis* and *C. pisifera* which can withstand hard frosts. *C. lawsoniana* is quite hardy, but can suffer damage during a particularly hard winter. *C. obtusa* is a more delicate species which is sensitive to severe frosts and to excessive heat and drought. There are several dwarf cultivars of this species, the smallest being 'Nana'; the slightly taller 'Nana Aurea' has yellow-tipped branches. *C. pisifera* requires greater humidity than the others. There is a wide range of cultivars varying in size and leaf colour. Some beautiful dwarf forms are 'Filifera Nana' and 'Nana Variegata' which has white variegation, and many others.

Cypresses need a humusy soil rich in nutrients and partially shaded position. They do poorly in full sun. They are propagated by cuttings taken in July and August. The species that do not root easily can be propagated by grafting on to *Chamaecyparis lawsoniana* in May and June.

1

The most frequently cultivated forms of *Chamaecyparis obtusa* include 'Nana Gracilis' (1). It has an irregular conical shape and attains a height of 6 ft (2 m) after many years. The thick branches form a sort of shell pattern (2) by their position. 'Nana Aurea' has needles with a golden sheen and grows slightly taller.

An interesting cultivar of a conical to globose shape, *Chamaecyparis pisifera* 'Boulevard' (3), has soft grey-green foliage. It grows slowly and can be recommended even for small rock gardens. It attains the best shape and coloration in moist sandy soil. The slower-growing and conspicuous 'Filifera Aurea' has long, thin, pendulous branches with scaly golden needles (4). It spreads into a wide cone. In case of a small rockery, preference should be given to the dwarfer 'Filifera Aurea Nana'.

2

4

3

Glory-of-the-snow
Chionodoxa luciliae
Liliaceae

Chionodoxas are attractive and undemanding bulbous plants native to the mountains of Asia Minor. They have a relatively small greyish-white bulb from which a few linear leaves and the stalk bearing several flowers grow in spring. The flowers are campanulate, composed of six petals. The fruit is a globular capsule.

The blossoms appear among the first early spring flowers. They emerge in March and die back by June. Chionodoxas are very beautiful and easy to cultivate. They prefer good, humus-rich soil and a moist situation. Several bulbs can be planted in a rockery, for example in the alpine meadow, or under shrubs. They are tolerant of both full sun and partial shade.

The bulbs are planted in autumn, 2 in (5 cm) deep and 2½ to 4 in (6.5 to 8 cm) apart. The plants are propagated from bulbils or seed sown immediately after ripening. They often naturalize themselves by self-sowing seeds. The seeds have a caruncle (fleshy protuberance) which is a delicacy for ants; thanks to the ants, the plants are often spread to various places in the garden.

Chionodoxa luciliae (1) has two to three linear, fluted leaves. From the centre grows the 4 to 6 in (10 to 15 cm) high stalk with several flowers measuring just over ½ in (1½ to 2 cm) across. The rich blue petals become white at the base. This species flowers in March and April. Besides the botanical species, there exist a few attractive forms, such as the white-flowered var. *alba* or var. *rosea* with white-centred pink blossoms. The cultivar 'Pink Giant' has a larger inflorescence and blue or pink flowers (2).

Chionodoxa sardensis (3) has smaller dark blue flowers. It also exists in white and pink-flowered varieties. All species of *Chionodoxa* can interbreed, and plants of mixed parentage are often encountered in gardens.

1

2

3

67

Daisy
Chrysanthemum arcticum

Compositae

The 600 species of the genus *Chrysanthemum* comprise both annual and perennial plants. Some are low, suited for rock gardens, but most are taller and highly ornamental. They have been crossbred into many beautiful cultivars, unfortunately unsuitable for rockeries.

The stems are terminated by a solitary capitulum. The aster-like flower consists of a central disc of usually yellow florets (3) surrounded by white ray florets (4), which are sometimes absent. The fruit is an achene without a pappus.

Daisies are grown in the sun in loamy soil rich in nutrients. They are undemanding and very attractive plants.

Propagation is by seed or division of clumps, preferably before May.

One of the more frequently cultivated rockery daisies is *Chrysanthemum arcticum* (1), a native of northern Europe, North America and northern Asia. It has creeping stems and deeply lobed leaves. The leaves on the lower part of the stem are petiolate. The large flower heads have yellow disc florets and white ray florets. The flowering stage is in October and November, at a time when flowers are scarce in gardens, which makes the species very welcome. It attains a height of up to 1 ft (30 cm), and should therefore be accommodated in a larger rockery or natural part of the garden. It spreads readily to form loose, ornamental carpets of dark green. It does not have to be lifted and divided too often and can remain in the same site for many years. Although it is entirely frost-resistant, it does not usually flower if planted in a frost pocket or in regions affected by early winters. The attractive cultivar 'Rosea' has pink ray florets.

The high mountains of Europe are the homeland of *Chrysanthemum alpinum* (2). It reaches a height of 4 to 6 in (10 to 15 cm); the palmatisect leaves forming the ground rosette are dark green above and grey-green below. The solitary flower heads are about 1 in (2.5 cm) across and are borne on straight, unbranched stalks. It flowers in July and August. Its natural habitat is acid rocks, stony plains and screes, in alpine regions and along the snow-line. An acid soil and a cool situation are also required, which makes cultivation difficult.

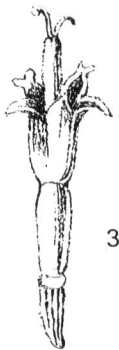

3

4

2

1

Alpine Clematis
Clematis alpina
Ranunculaceae

Some species of the genus *Clematis* have been for a long time attracting the interest of horticulturists. Multiple crossbreeding has given rise to many cultivars with large, prominent flowers of various colours ranging from white to red, dark blue and violet, classed under the name *C.* × *hybridum*. These plants are not suitable for rock gardens, but rather for covering pergolas, walls or fences.

Better suited to the rock garden are natural species. A mellow wall in the background can set them off. They are planted in sandy-loamy soil in the sun or semi-shade, in a sheltered situation. Apart from *Clematis alpina*, the best species to choose is the undemanding *C. montana* with fragrant white to pinkish flowers or its cultivar 'Rubens' with pink flowers. *C. tangutica* with large, yellow, perfumed blossoms can also create an attractive background effect. It flowers from June through to autumn and spreads heavily.

Clematis has an interesting flower structure. There are four coloured sepals replacing the corolla which is either underdeveloped or very inconspicuous. The flowers of some species are solitary and on long peduncles. The fruit is an achene with a long, feathery style (2, 4).

The species are propagated from seed, the cultivars by green cuttings taken in June and July.

Clematis alpina (1) is attractive when trained up trees or allowed to creep over rocks, eventually attaining a length of 10 ft (3 m). It produces blue bell-like flowers from May to July. In the wild it grows on rocks and screes, in thickets on the edges of forests, chiefly at alpine elevations, usually on limestone, from Europe to Siberia.

One of the best species, with ornamental flowers and fruits, is *Clematis macropetala* (3) from northern China, Manchuria and Siberia. It bears a profusion of flowers from May to June; the individual flowers measure up to 4 in (10 cm) across.

4

1

2

3

71

Autumn Crocus
Colchicum bornmuelleri

Liliaceae

The large and conspicuous flowers of colchicums appear in autumn. The genus *Colchicum* comprises some 60 species distributed mainly in the Mediterranean. The flowers are up to 8 in (20 cm) long, including the perianth forming a thin tube growing largely underground. The flowers are pinkish to violet-pink. Many cultivars with large flowers of more distinct colours including white have been developed. One of the most beautiful is the full-flowered 'Water Lily'. The improved forms are named *C.* × *hybridum.*

Two of the most frequently encountered garden species are *Colchicum bornmuelleri* and *C. autumnale.* They are grown in good-quality garden soil rich in nutrients. The corms are planted out when the leaves die back, early in autumn, 4 to 6 in (10 to 15 cm) deep according to the size. The planting must be followed by copious watering. With the exception of *C. autumnale* which tolerates damp ground, the other colchicums prefer a dry habitat in summer and should be set out in a sunny position.

Propagation is best by growing on the tiny cormlets which develop on the corm in sufficient numbers in good soil, often multiplying to such an extent that the plants stop flowering. The corms have to be dug out in July and planted separately. Botanical species can be propagated by seed.

Colchicum bornmuelleri (1) comes from Asia Minor. The pink buds become violet-pink as they open, the centre being white. The flowers are large and conspicuous.

5

The damp meadows and beech groves of Europe are the home of *Colchicum autumnale* (2). Several delicately violet-tinged flowers grow from one corm. Some cultivars are grown in gardens, such as 'Albiflorum' with tiny white flowers, the white double-flowered 'Albiplenum' or the violet, double-flowered 'Plenum'.

Colchicums grow from a corm in a brown leather covering, or tunic (3). Only the flowers appear in autumn, the leaves not emerging until the following spring. They are large and noticeable by their bright green colour (4). The triloculate capsule with globular seeds (5) is concealed among them near the ground. The leaves wither in late summer, but they cannot be cut off as to do so would weaken the corms.

73

Fumitory
Corydalis cheilanthifolia — Papaveraceae

There are about 90 species of fumitories. Almost all have finely dissected leaves and distinctly symmetrical spurred flowers held in loose racemes. The fruit is a short capsule. They are mostly shade-loving plants, easy to cultivate. Their natural habitat is light woodland, so they should therefore be placed in a wooded part or underneath shrubs. They succeed in open, humus-rich soil in a moist situation.

Propagation is by seed, immediately after ripening. The seeds germinate readily and under favourable conditions fumitories tend to sow themselves freely. To prevent overmultiplication, cut off the dead flowers before the seeds become mature.

A spring-flowering plant of light, humus-rich woodland of central Europe is the Fingered Fumitory or *Corydalis solida* (3). It has a small yellowish tuber (4), grey-green leaves and deep violet-pink, very occasionally white flowers. It flowers in March and April. Of similar appearance is the Hollow Fumitory, *C. cava,* which differs in having a hollow tuber (5) and undivided leaves underneath the flowers. Both species form large growths. *C. cheilanthifolia* and *C. lutea* are the two species most commonly grown in rock gardens.

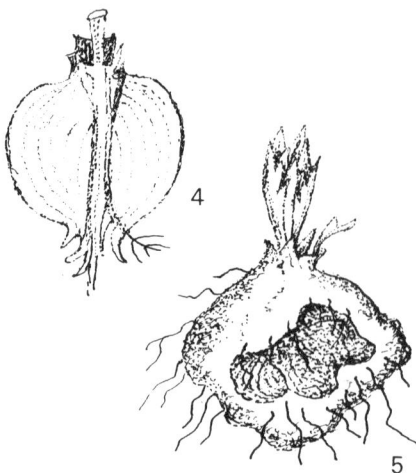

Corydalis cheilanthifolia (1) is an interesting species, 8 to 12 in (20 to 30 cm) tall and native to China. The pale green leaves are very finely dissected, similar to the fronds of ferns. They persist throughout winter when they assume a slight bronze sheen. The flowering period is in April and May. The flowers are yellow and inconspicuous, so that the chief ornamental effect is produced by the foliage. The plant dies down if exposed to excessive winter moisture, so it should therefore be protected.

Corydalis lutea (2) from southern Europe is undemanding but can become a nuisance due to its habit of self-sowing. This fresh-looking plant forms dense rounded clumps, 8 to 12 in (20 to 30 cm) high, of bright green, finely-divided leaves and numerous stems with short racemes of pure yellow flowers which appear from spring through to autumn. The fruit is a siliqua-like capsule containing glossy black seeds.

1

2

3

75

Herringbone Cotoneaster
Cotoneaster horizontalis

Rosaceae

Cotoneasters are deciduous woody plants of various shapes including creeping and low-growing species or species attaining a height of up to 10 ft (3 m). Species can be deciduous, semi-deciduous or evergreen. The tiny white to pinkish flowers are solitary or arranged in inflorescences. The fruits are small globular pomes, red or black in colour.

Cotoneasters will grow well in ordinary, well-drained garden soil in a sunny position. They do better in dry situations than in ones that are too moist. The space taken up by a full-grown specimen should be taken into account when planting cotoneasters in a rock garden.

The creeping species are easily propagated. Any young branches laying on the ground take root readily and can then be detached and planted. Cuttings of half-ripened wood can also be taken for all species in June and July. Most species can be propagated by layering in spring.

Cotoneaster horizontalis is a deciduous shrub from China. It is often cultivated in gardens, especially against a wall or a steep bank, but it is unsuitable for small rockeries because of its wide-spreading growth. This shrub has the distinctive herringbone branch structure which gives it its common name. From May to July it produces small pale pink flowers (2) and in autumn it is ornamented by abundant red berries (1).

The creeping species of *Cotoneaster* include the evergreen *C. dammeri* (3).

The white to pink flowers appear in May. It is only 4 to 6 in (10 to 15 cm) high, but it spreads fast thanks to its long trailing branches. It is a native of China.

The evergreen *Cotoneaster microphyllus* (4) reaches a maximum height of 30 in (75 cm) and is a beautiful species suitable for small rock gardens. The leaves are tiny with convex margins. A profusion of small white flowers appears in May. It is native to the Himalayas and China. It is quite hardy.

3

4

The mountains of New Zealand are the home of several species of the genus *Cotula.* Some succeed in the European environment, others are difficult to cultivate. Some other species are also native to South America and South Africa.

Only a few species are encountered in rock gardens. They are predominantly creeping plants, and their trailing stems spread and take root to form an extensive carpet. The stems are leafy, the leaves are alternate and palmatisect. The unimpressive flowers are clustered at the end of thin stalks.

Cotulas thrive in loamy, humus-rich soil with good drainage. They can be planted both in the sun and shade. They are undemanding plants which can serve as a substitute for lawn or can be planted between bulbous plants, to fill their place after flowering is over.

They can be propagated easily by pieces of rooted stem cut off after flowering.

Cotula squalida (1) is only 1 to 2 in (2.5 to 5 cm) tall. Since it spreads freely, it can be used as an excellent ground cover between stepping stones or steps. It tolerates being trampled upon but will not flower. In any case, its flowers are inconspicuous and it is grown chiefly for the dark green leaves with a brown sheen.

Cotula potentillina (2) is of similar appearance, but has finer textured, olive-green foliage turning brown in autumn.

Cotula pectinata var. *wilcoxii* (3) is less hardy but more ornamental than the previous species; its tiny yellow flowers are arranged in a flat capitulum. Its flowering stage begins in early summer and lasts for a long time. The capitulum then turns brown. This lovely rock garden

2

1

plant from the New Zealand mountains is
still rarely seen in rockeries.
It requires good drainage, an acid, sandy
soil, and a place in the sun. Sunscorch can
be a problem and it is intolerant of
waterlogged soil or permanent dampness
around the stems and leaves. It should,
therefore, be surrounded by pebbles and
protected in winter by a pane of glass.

3

Crocus chrysanthus

Crocuses are probably present in every garden. They are cormous plants with conspicuous large flowers of various colours. They have narrow, grass-like foliage with a silvery central stripe and grow in a rosette either in autumn or spring, according to the species. They start to develop fully only after flowering is over. The flowers are composed of six petals fused into a tube at the base. Some species produce flowers in early spring like *Crocus chrysanthus,* others in late spring or autumn.

The majority of species are natives of the Mediterranean. The hillside and mountain meadows of Europe are the natural habitat of *Crocus heuffelianus* with its large violet or sometimes white flowers.

Crocuses require good drainage, open soil rich in humus, and a site in the sun. During their dormant period they prefer a dry environment. The corms of spring-flowering species are planted in September and October; those of autumn-flowering species are set out by mid-August, 3 to 4 in (5 to 8 cm) deep. It is advisable to group several corms of one species together to obtain the best display.

Crocuses are propagated by cormlets. Species can also be propagated by seed, but this is a much slower method. In addition to natural species, there are many beautiful cultivars. It is, however, better to plant the species in rock gardens; their flowers are smaller and more delicate.

The yellow-flowered species include *Crocus chrysanthus* (1), a native of south-eastern Europe and Asia Minor.

3

A single corm produces several flowers in February and March.

Crocus tommasinianus (2) has slender violet flowers with white throats and long perianth tubes. It produces a wealth of flowers in February and March and often tends to sow itself. It is easily naturalized and so can be set out in grass. It is a native of Dalmatia.

September and October are the flowering months for *Crocus speciosus.* It has a relatively large, globular corm with thin, pale brown skin which disintegrates from around the base (3). The large, violet-blue flower has darker venation and a white centre. The stigma is orange and much divided (4). This is one of the most beautiful species of *Crocus* and is native to the Balkans and Asia Minor.

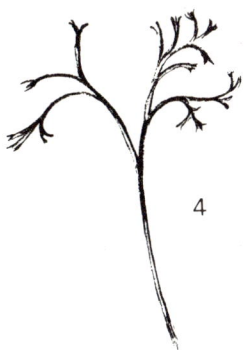

4

1

2

81

Sowbread
Cyclamen purpurascens Primulaceae

Everybody is familiar with the striking, large-flowered florists' cyclamen grown in pots. The small-flowered species cultivated in gardens, however, are much lovelier. They have a large, flattened tuber which produces roots at different places according to species. The leaves, arranged in a rosette, are dark green, petiolate, entire or serrate, often slightly violet on the underside. Some species have a silvery pattern above. The flowers come in the complete range of pinks with a darker eye. The petals are recurved and the fruit is a globular capsule. Several species are cultivated in rock gardens, but not all are sufficiently resistant to harsh winters. *Cyclamen purpurascens* does not require protection in winter.

Cyclamens are planted in a mixture of turf and leaf mould with a supplement of crushed or ground limestone or old plaster. They are placed in semi-shade, in well-drained soil. They are intolerant of waterlogging even if only for a very short period. In autumn, the soil should be improved with well-rotted compost. They are planted in the dormant period, some 2 to 4 in (5 to 10 cm) deep. If possible, they should not be transplanted in order to keep them in bloom.

Propagation is by sowing seed as soon as it is ripe. They germinate well but produce flowers only after several years, when the tuber has grown bigger.

Cyclamen purpurascens (1), also called 'alpine violet', a native of central and southern Europe, flowers from July to September. The tubers produce roots on the sides and sometimes reach a diameter of 6 in (15 cm). The species has carmine flowers and there is an attractive white-flowered variety.

Cyclamen coum (2) is an early spring flowerer. The tubers take root on the underside, and the dark green leaves appear in autumn. Any winter protection has to be removed in early spring. Cultivars with white to dark pink blossoms are common.

The ornamental leaves of *Cyclamen neapolitanum* (3) resemble those of the ivy *Hedera helix* and the species is consequently also known as *C. hederifolium.* It produces a profusion of pink flowers, (white in var. *album* [4]), in September and October. The leaves form a beautiful ground cover after flowering. The tubers form roots on the upper side, and have to be planted 4 in (10 cm) deep. This species requires plenty of sunshine and a warm, dry and sheltered site.

Broom
Cytisus decumbens

Leguminosae

Brooms are deciduous shrubs of various shapes, ranging from low, creeping shrubs to ones 3 to 6 ft (1 to 2 m) high. They usually have single or trifoliate small leaves. Brooms all have the pea-like flowers, which are a feature of the whole family Leguminosae (formerly Papilionaceae). The blooms are symmetrical, with a large upper petal, the so-called standard, two narrow, elongate petals, or wings, and two small, lower petals forming the keel. The fruit is a flat pod, known as a legume, containing several seeds.

Brooms do well in sandy garden soil which does not have to be rich in nutrients. They are fond of sunny situations where they produce a profusion of flowers. They are mostly resistant to cold. Some beautiful cultivars with blossoms of various colours (even bi-coloured ones) require a sheltered site.

Botanical species propagate by seed, cultivars by softwood cuttings taken immediately after flowering has ended. Creeping species are best propagated by layering of stems which readily take root.

Cytisus decumbens (1) is a low-growing shrub, only 4 to 8 in (10 to 20 cm) high. It spreads readily and soon covers a large space. The branches are long, thin and trailing, covered with small leaves, hairy on both sides. It produces large golden-yellow flowers in May and June. The fruit is a legume (2). It can be used in a large rock garden, on the top of a terrace or dry wall, where the overhanging branches form a cascade of yellow blossoms.

One of the larger shrubs is *Cytisus* × *praecox* (3), up to 6 ft (2 m) high and wide, with slightly pendulous, thin branches. Its pale yellow, fragrant flowers appear in April. It is also suited for large rockeries or as a specimen plant.

The Common Broom, *Cytisus scoparius* (*Sarothamnus scoparius*) (4), is 2 to 6 ft (60 cm to 2 m) tall, having small trifoliate leaves on angular green branches. It flowers in May and June. It can also be planted in an extensive rock garden or as an effective specimen plant. It is not suitable for small rockeries.

Garland Flower
Daphne cneorum   Thymelaeaceae

Daphnes are hardy shrubs coming in a variety of shapes and sizes. In spring, they brighten the rock garden by a profusion of mostly pink, fragrant flowers. The species native to the humus-rich woodlands of central Europe is the Mezereon, *Daphne mezereum,* a shrub attaining a height of 3 ft (1 m). The pink flowers appear in clusters on long branches before the leaves develop. In autumn it is ornamented by bright red but poisonous fruits. It is a rare plant in the wild and strictly protected. It is illegal to pick this plant or lift it to transplant into the garden.

Some low-growing, profusely flowering species can be cultivated in small rock gardens. All species are propagated by seed from which the pulp is removed first. Some species can also be propagated by cuttings in June and July. The species *Daphne blagayana, D. cneorum* and *D. arbuscula* can be propagated by layering in June and July. One of the lower branches is partially cut through, dusted with hormone rooting powder and bent down so the cut area rests in the soil. Cover with a stone to hold the branch down until good roots are formed. Then the new plant can be severed from its parent.

3

Daphne cneorum (1) is a beautiful compact evergreen shrub, only 6 to 12 in (15 to 30 cm) high. It has trailing, leafy branches terminated by large umbels of pink, fragrant flowers, appearing in May and June. Another flowering period often follows in August and September. No fruits are produced even under the best conditions. In the rock garden, it is set out in the sun or in a partially shaded place in humus-rich soil. It requires good drainage and is suitable for any rock garden.

Daphne arbuscula (2) is an evergreen shrub, 4 to 8 in (10 to 20 cm) high, with trailing, leafy branches. It flowers later than *D. cneorum*. Since it does not form

fruits in cultivation, it is propagated by layering or by cuttings. It is suitable even for smaller rockeries.

Daphne blagayana (3) has creeping branches covered with bright green, persistent leaves. The branches are terminated by dense umbels of creamy-yellow, strong-scented blooms. It starts flowering in February and the blossoms often persist until April. It thrives among acid rocks like granite, in semi-shade. Under favourable conditions it will cover a large area. The new shoots should be cut back after flowering, or the older branches tend to become leafless.

Alpine Pink
Dianthus alpinus

Caryophyllaceae

Pinks are present in almost every rock garden. Every grower can choose from this large genus according to various requirements: species suitable for a large rock garden or a miniature rockery, varieties with white, pink or red flowers, small or large, single or double and usually pleasantly scented. The fruit is a capsule (4).

The genus *Dianthus* covers about 300 species distributed chiefly in Europe, Siberia and Japan. They include annual and perennial species, low-growing and tall. Some are quite undemanding, grow well and spread to form large, profusely flowering cushions. Others are difficult to cultivate. All require well-drained, sandy soil rich in humus, and a sunny position.

Propagation is by division or cuttings; the seed of species can be sown in May and June.

The Alpine Pink, *Dianthus alpinus* (1), is one of the more delicate species. The beautiful large flowers are marked in the middle by a purplish, white-dotted ring. This lovely plant has to be situated in the most favourable position to feel at home.

It is a native of the limestone Alps, where it is confined to heights of up to 6,500 ft (almost 2,000 m). That is the reason why it often does not succeed in rock gardens. It does best on screes. There is also a white-flowered cultivar called *D. alpinus* 'Albus'.

Dianthus glacialis (2) forms beautiful, dark green, compact cushions, only 1 to 2 in (2½ to 5 cm) high. The reddish-pink flowers lack the dark pattern on the base. It blooms from May to July or even into August. Its habitats are the mountains of central Europe, where it occurs in the sub-alpine and alpine regions on screes or in rocky crevices, often on an acid substrate. It should be planted in a rocky cleft with good drainage or on scree slopes turned away from the sun. It is hardier than *D. alpinus*, but not very persistent either. It is easily propagated by seed.

One of the fragile, profusely flowering, small-sized pinks is *Dianthus subacaulis* (3). Its narrow, greyish blue-green leaves form firm cushions. The double-flowered cultivar is particularly lovely. This species is quite undemanding and easy to cultivate.

4

2

3

1

Yellow Whitlow Grass
Draba aizoides

Drabas comprise a large number of mainly mountain species found in all the continents except Australia and Africa. They are restricted to high elevations, up to the snow line, and to arctic regions. They are attractive, low-growing alpine plants, but unfortunately they are not well known in cultivation. The leaf rosettes make dense, more or less firm cushions. Most species produce yellow flowers, only some are white. Some species have large blossoms, others are small-flowered, but the flower always consists of four petals and four sepals, which is typical of all the species of the family Cruciferae. The inflorescence is a raceme, the fruit is a siliqua.

Drabas require poor, gravelly soil and ample sunshine. Good drainage is the main prerequisite of successful cultivation, as excessive moisture is harmful.

Propagation is by seed sown in February or by division of clumps after the flowering period is over in July. Propagation by cuttings in August is also possible.

3

Draba aizoides (1) is restricted to the alpine elevations of the European mountains where it grows mainly on limestone rocks. It has dense basal rosettes composed of stiff linear leaves, bristly on the margins. The stem is glabrous, 2 to 4 in (5 to 10 cm) tall, terminated by a raceme of four to fifteen golden-yellow flowers. The petals are slightly notched; the fruits are broadly elongated siliquas.

Draba alpina (2) makes firm cushions. This plant, native to the northern regions of Eurasia, sometimes has a hairy stem, up to 8 in (20 cm) high, and racemes of four to ten flowers. The flowering period is in June.

The smallest species of the genus is *Draba bryoides* var. *imbricata* (3), suitable for miniature rockeries. The numerous short stems bear tiny overlapping scale-like leaves. The leaf rosettes are about $\frac{1}{8}$ in (2 mm) across and form compact cushions out of which thin stems, 1 in (2.5 cm) high with two to four yellow flowers grow in May. The native habitat of this plant is the Caucasus.

The attractive, undemanding hybrid *Draba* × *suendermannii* (4), about 2 in (5 cm) high, has a profusion of white flowers in March and April. It can be used successfully in small rockeries or trough gardens.

Mountain Avens
Dryas octopetala   Rosaceae

One of the best-known and most attractive woody plants of alpine regions is the Mountain Avens. It grows on screes and rocks in the high European mountains and in arctic regions. The trailing branches bear alternate, smallish and highly decorative, leathery leaves, which are 1 in (2.5 cm) long, glabrous and dark green above, grey-felted below, with a regularly crenate margin.

Cultivation in gardens is relatively easy. Although in the wild the Mountain Avens is confined mostly to basic rocks, it can be successfully grown on an acid substrate. It can be damaged by frost in winter, but it usually regenerates in the spring. It is planted in gravelly, humus-rich soil, in the sun or semi-shade. The twigs lying on the ground take root readily and make the plants spread into beautiful, dark green carpets.

Dryas octopetala succeeds in gardens, but usually flowers less profusely than in the mountains because it lacks the mountain climate. Preference is therefore given to D. × *suendermannii* (hybrid of *D. octopetala* and *D. drummondii*). This plant is more robust than *D. octopetala* and its buds are yellowish.

Propagation is by division of the rooted twigs. The seeds are sown immediately after they have ripened. The cuttings usually take root only with difficulty.

2

Dryas octopetala (1) bears large, striking flowers, measuring up to 1½ in (4 cm) across, from June to August. The flowers grow solitarily on stalks 2 to 4 in (5 to 10 cm) high. They have six to nine white petals and a large number of stamens. The Mountain Avens remains ornamental in the fruiting period. The ovaries ripen into achenes, each terminated by a long, feathery style. The fruit is attractive, hairy and globular (2), similar to the fruit of pulsatillas.

Of much smaller size is *Dryas octopetala* var. *tenella* (3), which is considered by some experts as an independent species, *D. tenella*. It is a slow grower, suited to small rockeries. The fruit is also considerably smaller (4).

1

3

4

Edraianthus, also known as *Hedraeanthus* and mentioned in catalogues under the name of *Wahlenbergia,* is one of the most beautiful
rock garden plants. The natural distribution of this relatively small
genus is mainly in Dalmatia and on the Balkan Peninsula and
around the Mediterranean. All species have narrow leaves, more or
less hairy. The usually bluish-violet, campanulate flowers are either
solitary (*E. pumilio, E. dinaricus, E. serpyllifolius*) or arranged in terminal heads (*E. dalmaticus, E. graminifolius, E. tenuifolius*). In the
wild they grow on limestone, predominantly in rocky crevices, forming compact cushions or dense clumps.

In the garden they have to be planted in well-drained soil. They do
well in full sun, in humus-rich, stony, calcareous soil, preferably between stones or on a dry wall. The site should be carefully planned
because the plants have a long tap root and older specimens cannot
be transplanted.

Propagation is by seed sown in February, or by cuttings. They tend
to be self-sown in suitable situations.

1

2

Edraianthus pumilio (1), a native of Dalmatia, has needle-like, grey-green leaves, about ¾ in (2 cm) long, arranged in dense rosettes. The flowers are solitary, on very short stalks, upturned, almost sessile on the grey-green cushion. The colour and shape of the flowers is reminiscent of bellflowers. It blooms profusely in June and July. The whole flowering plant is 1½–2¼ in (4 to 6 cm) tall.

Edraianthus graminifolius (2) has clustered flowers. The leaves are narrow, linear, dark green, 2¼ to 4 in (6 to 10 cm)

long, growing from a dense clump. The stems are trailing, up to 6 in (15 cm) long, arranged in a circle and decumbent at the tips. The inflorescence — an umbel — is composed of three to seven bluish-violet campanulate flowers. The points of the corolla are recurved. The flowering period is in July and August. This species is native to Italy, the Balkans and the south-eastern Carpathians. It is easy to cultivate in a sunny position on a limestone substrate with good drainage. Because of its long trailing stems, it has to be provided with a spacious site.

Winter Aconite
Eranthis hyemalis

Ranunculaceae

Eranthis should not be absent from any garden. Its large, golden-yellow flowers and decorative, bright green foliage appear already in late winter and become the first signs of the coming spring.

From the dark brown, irregular tuberous rhizome (4) grow several stems terminated by single, large, yellow blossoms. The corolla is simulated by the calyx composed of five to eight rich yellow sepals, while the corolla itself is modified into small glands. Around the stem just below the flowers is a ruff of deeply divided leaves, arranged in whorls. They are very attractive even in the fruiting season. The bright green leaves develop after flowering.

The plants are usually set out in larger numbers underneath shrubs or trees, but they also succeed in the rock garden. They require humus-rich soil and a moist situation in the sun or semi-shade. The tubers are planted in early autumn, 2 to 2¾ in (5 to 7 cm) deep.

Eranthis is easily propagated by seed sown immediately on ripening. The seed germinates readily, and in favourable positions the plants tend to multiply by sowing themselves. To prevent this, the faded heads have to be removed. Once every two or three years, the plants should be lifted and propagated by lateral tubers. The tubers look like lumps of earth and the small ones can be overlooked unless the soil is sieved.

One of the first early-spring flowers is *Eranthis hyemalis* (1). It is 4 to 6 in (10 to 15 cm) tall and appears in February, often producing its large yellow flowers while the snow is still on the ground. Its natural habitat covers mainly southern Europe, but it also reaches central Europe.

Eranthis cilicica (2) comes from Greece and Asia Minor. It attains a height of 4 in (10 cm) and its flowers are larger than in *E. hyemalis.* The budding leaves are reddish-purple, extremely fine and deeply lobed. The stem leaves below the flowers are divided into narrow segments. It blooms about a fortnight later than the previous species; it is shorter and slightly less vigorous.

The fruit of *Eranthis* is decorative. The follicles with seeds open into the shape of a star supported by the green stem leaves (3).

Fleabane
Erigeron uniflorus   Compositae

The genus *Erigeron* includes many species of various shapes and sizes, distributed throughout Europe, North and South America and Australia. Erigerons are annual or perennial, tall or low-growing. Among the dwarfer species suitable for rock gardens are *E. alpinus, E. uniflorus, E. leiomerus, E. neglectus,* and *E. humilis.* The taller species and a number of garden cultivars are grown in flower beds. Erigerons bear a great resemblance to asters, the botanical difference being in the position of the pappus on achenes, which in the former is arranged in one row and in asters, in two to three rows. Botanical species have showy inflorescences but the flower heads are relatively small. Low-growing species have large flowers in proportion to their height. The ray florets are mostly pinkish-violet to white. These are undemanding plants and easy to cultivate, doing well in ordinary garden soil and a sunny situation. Propagation is by seed or division.

The low-growing species include *Erigeron uniflorus* (1), which is only 1½ to 3 in (4 to 8 cm) tall. It has entire leaves, glabrous with a bristly margin, arranged in a rosette. The bracts are tinged with scarlet. It flowers from July to September. In the wild it inhabits the higher mountain regions of Europe and North America, chiefly in stony areas. In the garden it requires a moist situation but is intolerant of damp and must therefore be covered in the winter months. It forms large clumps under favourable conditions, and sometimes sows itself.

2

Erigeron leiomerus (3) has narrow, lanceolate, entire leaves in a ground rosette. The stem 2¾ to 4 in (7 to 10 cm) tall, are terminated by large flowerheads, up to ¾ in (2 cm) across. This species produces a wealth of flowers throughout the summer. It often produces self-sown seedlings.

Erigeron humilis (2) is even lower-growing than *E. uniflorus*. The entire lanceolate leaves form a rosette of only 1½ in (4 cm) across. From its centre grows a ¾ in (2 cm) high, hairy stem with a large solitary flower head, up to ¾ in (2 cm) across. The ray florets are filamentous, pale violet; the disc florets are yellowish-brown. The bracts are densely covered with hairs. It does best on east-facing banks of the rock garden in acid leafmould. It should be topdressed with fine gravel as a protection against damp, and covered in winter.

3

1

Dog's Tooth Violet
Erythronium dens-canis   Liliaceae

Erythronium is a beautiful bulbous plant distributed predominantly in North America. A single species, *E. dens-canis,* is found in Europe. The bulb produces several stalked, elongated to elliptical leaves, often marbled, and one to several stems terminated by a solitary flower, or in some species two to four pendulous flowers ranging in colour from almost white to pinkish-violet. There are six petals with recurved points and six pronounced stamens emerging from each flower. The fruit is a capsule containing very fine seeds.

Erythroniums, originally woodland plants, should be cultivated in well-drained, loamy soil with an acid pH. They are planted out in August, 2¼ to 3 in (6 to 8 cm) deep, in light shade. It is advisable not to transplant them as they take a long time to adjust to a new site and start flowering again. The bulbs have no outer coating and when transplanting is imperative, they should be kept in peat or moistened soil to prevent them from drying out. Artificial fertilizers must be avoided but some well-rotted compost can be added to the soil. Only *E. dens-canis* is completely hardy and survives the winter without any cover.

Erythroniums are propagated by bulbils in August. Botanical species can be propagated from the seed which is sown immediately after ripening. The plants grown from seeds flower within three to four years.

The only European species, the Dog's Tooth Violet (1), is found in clear, humus-rich woodland. Its occurrence in nature is diminishing and it is a strictly protected species. The bulb (2) is reminiscent of a dog's tooth which gave rise to the plant's name. A single pink fragrant flower appears in March or April at the end of a leafless 4 to 8 in (10 to 20 cm) tall stem. The plant begins to wither in May. Many cultivars have been produced.

Erythronium oregonum (3) has rich green, yellow-veined leaves. The stem is up to 14 in (35 cm) tall and bears several whitish-yellow flowers with a brown central ring in April and May. It has bigger bulbs than the other species and so must be planted rather deeper. It requires a winter cover. Its beautiful cultivar 'White Beauty' with large flowers is often cultivated, and sometimes related to the species *E. revolutum.*

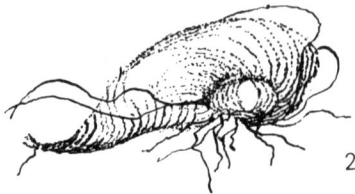

2

1

3

Spurge, Milkwort
Euphorbia myrsinites   Euphorbiaceae

Out of some 600 species of *Euphorbia,* only a few are grown in gardens, and the selection is even more limited for rock gardens. Euphorbias cover annual and perennial plants, semi-shrubs and shrubs. They seek predominantly dry situations all over the world; some resemble cacti. When damaged, the plants exude a white, milky juice. The flowers are inconspicuous, very small, but their effect is replaced by the impressive yellow to orange leaves.

In addition to *Euphorbia myrsinites* and *E. capitulata,* another species encountered in rock gardens is *E. polychroma* (*E. epithymoides*), forming beautiful, up to 20 in (50 cm) tall, dense, spherical clumps. The stems are covered with soft-haired leaves. The rich yellow bracts become orange in the autumn. This steppe plant is recommended for large rock gardens or as a solitary plant.

Euphorbias are hardy and can be grown in full sun, in standard, well-drained, stony garden soil. They are propagated by division, cuttings, and the easiest method is by seed. They tend to produce self-sown seedlings which are found far from the mother plant. The seeds are frequently dispersed by ants which are fond of the fleshy excrescence (caruncle) which is present.

2

Euphorbia myrsinites (1) has stems, 7 to 10 in (18 to 25 cm) long, which are prostrate at the base but then grow erect. It has dense foliage which makes the non-flowering stems look like green cones with open scales (2). In May to July the stems are terminated by fairly large but inconspicuous inflorescences. The stems spread to all sides, and so sufficient space has to be planned for when the plants are set out. The old stems lose foliage at the base and should be removed in early spring.

Euphorbia capitulata (3), a native of Dalmatia and Greece, has long, trailing stems, densely covered with small, bluish-green leaflets, and forms a low decorative carpet. The stems are terminated by small yellow inflorescences. The underground, thread-like offshoots spread far and wide, often grow underneath large stones and invade other plants. This is prevented by setting out this species in a suitable site where it has room to spread and can easily be controlled.

1

3

When laying out the rock garden, grasses should not be forgotten. Their airy but striking appearance makes them a good foil to many features in the garden. Grasses comprise low-growing species, tall ones suitable as solitary plants, silvery-foliaged species (e. g. *F. cinerea)*, and species in various shades of green or with variegated leaf blades.

Grasses are pollinated by the wind and their flowers are adapted accordingly: the stamens consist of mobile anthers attached at their centres to long filaments which move slightly in the wind.

The genus *Festuca* is rich in species showing a variety of shapes. Some low-growing species form large cushions like *F. scoparia*. Others are tall and form clumps and are set out as solitary plants, like *F. gigantea*, which attains a height of 5 ft (150 cm). The inflorescence is a panicle of spikelets (4) with one or a number of flowers (5). The fruit is a grain. Grasses thrive in well-drained soil in a sunny position.

Festuca cinerea (1) is one of the most popular grasses. It is particularly beautiful in the flowering period when it looks as if made of lace. The flower stalks are erect, longer than leaves, terminated by a panicle of spikelets with yellow-orange anthers. It grows in the wild in warm sunny areas of the stony rocky regions of Europe. It is best planted in a well-drained or dry spot in the rockery or heath garden, where its silvery colour is particularly attractive. It should be divided every three to four years.

The beautiful, silvery blue-green colour of the foliage is the basic feature of *Festuca punctoria* (2). It has thin but tough prickly leaves and reaches a height of 4 to 6 in (10 to 15 cm). The flowers held on short stalks emerge in June and July. It is highly decorative and suitable even for small rockeries, but again, it has to be divided every few years.

The Pyrenees are the home of the low-growing *Festuca scoparia* (*F. crinum-ursi*) (3). It has pale green, fine-textured foliage, 2 to 4 in (5 to 8 cm) long. It forms large cushions after some time and it flourishes both in the sun and partial shade.

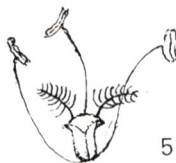

4   5

1

2

3

Snake's Head Fritillary
Fritillaria meleagris   Liliaceae

Fritillarias are pretty bulbous plants, varying in height. They have been cultivated since the Middle Ages. Some 100 species of this genus grow in the temperate zone of the Northern Hemisphere, with Asia Minor as the main area of distribution.

They require a rich, slightly sandy loam but not one that has been freshly fertilized. They like sunshine or partial shade. They should not be planted in the vicinity of shallow-rooting woody plants. They die back early and can therefore be planted below some carpeting plant. They can be left alone for several years. When transplanting, the bulbs are lifted after the foliage has died back and stored in peat to prevent them from drying out. They must be handled with care because damaged bulbs are prone to diseases. Fritillarias are set out in August; small bulbs are planted 3 in (8 cm) deep, large ones about 6 in (15 cm) deep.

Propagation is by bulbils or seed immediately after ripening. The seed germinates readily and the plants flower within three to four years. They become self-sown under favourable conditions.

5

Fritillaria meleagris (1), called the Snake's Head Fritillary, has an interesting flower with chequered petals. The flowers appear singly (rarely two to three) on the erect stem in April or May. The plant dies back by June. The bulb consists of several fleshy white scales (2). The fruit is a capsule (3) with flattened seeds. This species is native to Great Britain and central Europe. It has been disappearing steadily from its natural habitats and is therefore strictly protected by law. Many varieties have been cultivated, such as the white-flowered 'Aphrodite' (4), the dark 'Charon' and 'Poseidon' with a pronounced pink-chequered pattern.

Of a more robust and striking appearance is *Fritillaria pallidiflora* (5).

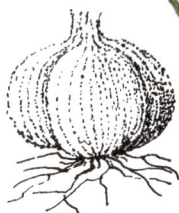

3

4

2

1

It has a considerably larger bulb and
attains a height of up to 20 in (50 cm).
The stem bears eight to twenty-five
leaves; from the axils of the top leaves
three to nine short-stalked, yellowish
flowers appear in April. The bulbs are
planted 4 in (10 cm) deep.

Gentian
Gentiana sino-ornata   Gentianaceae

Gentians are indispensable in the rock garden. Some species are noticeable by their large blue flowers, as is the most frequently cultivated Trumpet Gentian, *Gentiana acaulis* (this name covers a whole range of similar species). Most gentians have blue flowers, although white-, yellow- and violet-flowering species also exist. The flowering period differs according to species. A careful selection will allow you to enjoy flowering gentians from spring to autumn; autumn-flowering gentians include *G. sino-ornata*. The genus embraces over 900 annual and perennial species of various shapes and sizes. Some are only 2 in (5 cm) tall, others climb to a height of 6 ft (2 m). The stems are erect or prostrate, some forming attractive clumps, others thick carpets.

Gentians occur all over the world except in Africa. Some grow in the mountains, others in lowlands, some seek the dry steppes and others are found in stony grasslands, screes, pastures, mountain plateaus, sparse woodland, humid meadows or even peatbogs. They therefore differ in their requirements. Most gentians are propagated by seed, but some by division or cuttings.

Gentiana sino-ornata (1) produces flowers in late autumns. Its trailing, densely-leaved stems make roots and under favourable conditions form large green carpets. It is planted in humus-rich, acid soil. It is a good idea to plant it as a cover for bulbous plants, because it requires shade in spring, which is provided by the leaves of the bulbous plants. When these die back, it can again enjoy the sunshine.

The small Spring Gentian, *Gentiana verna* (2) blooms in early spring. The growths of this remarkably blue species are known from the wild, but its cultivation often fails. It is confined to the mountains of Europe and Siberia and their foothills. In the rock garden it should be situated in a place away from direct sun. It needs moist soil, and humus-rich garden soil supplemented with crumbled sphagnum moss which holds moisture around the roots.

Gentiana septemfida (3) flowers in summer. It is not very demanding and does well in any garden soil, in a situation away from direct sun. The often cultivated variety *lagodechiana* has trailing stems with ascending tips.

3

1

Crane's-bill
Geranium dalmaticum   Geraniaceae

Crane's-bills include various types of plants, from low-growing *Geranium dalmaticum* to tall ones (up to 32 in — 80 cm). Some form clumps, others form tubers like *G. tuberosum.* The genus includes weedy and small-flowered species, as well as some pretty rock garden plants. They have decorative, petiolate, more or less deeply divided palmate leaves. The five-petalled flowers are mostly in varying shades of pink. Crane's-bills have an interesting fruit resembling the bill of a crane, hence the common name. The styles grow together to form a long 'bill' which after ripening divides into five segments, each containing a seed. Drought makes the seeds shoot out forcefully (4) and disperse over a considerable distance.

Crane's-bills are easily propagated by seed. They are sown in February or March, and the seedlings can be set out in the rockery in autumn. In early spring or autumn, propagation can be by division.

4

Geranium dalmaticum (1), only 3 to 5 in (8 to 13 cm) tall, is suitable for rock gardens. It soon makes large cushions which remain decorative throughout the year. It flowers from July to August, and in autumn the leaves turn red. A lovely form with white flowers is also cultivated. The plants do well in standard garden soil to which some extra gravel has been added to give good drainage. They prefer a sunny situation.

Geranium sessiliflorum var. *nigrum* (2) comes from Australia and New Zealand. It has rounded, long-stalked brown leaves arranged in a rosette up to 8 in (20 cm) across. It flowers from July to October, sometimes longer. It is an undemanding and hardy plant which should be placed in a sunny spot in a crevice between stones or on a scree. It may spread by self-sowing but it is not invasive. Older specimens cannot be transplanted because of their taproot.

Attractive crane's-bills also include the
European Bloody Crane's-bill, *Geranium
sanguineum* (3). It is decorative both in
its large, carmine-pink flowers appering
from May to August, and in its bright
green, deeply-cut palmate leaves which
turn a striking red in autumn. It is about
18 in (45 cm) tall and therefore suited to
larger rock gardens. Two lower-growing
cultivars, 'Nanum' and 'Lancastriense',
are also often cultivated.

111

Chalk Plant
Gypsophila repens

Caryophyllaceae

Chalk plants are profusely flowering, undemanding plants. The genus embraces some 100 species, out of which one half is distributed in Europe and Asia. They are annual or perennial plants with branching stems and opposite, narrow, greyish leaves. The tiny flowers are arranged in corymbs or panicles according to species. The corolla is pink or white, with shallowly lobed petals. The fruit is a capsule.

Chalk plants are not particular as regards site, but they do best in full sun, in porous alkaline soil with good drainage. They become more compact under these conditions, and produce more flowers.

Propagation is by division, preferably in October, or by cuttings in May or June. The seeds are sown in April.

Gypsophila repens (1) is an undemanding, much-branched plant with a woody rootstock. It has trailing, sometimes red-tinged stems. It produces masses of flowers from June to August, but it is equally decorative by its grey-green foliage. It looks most attractive planted on a dry wall or by a large stone in the rockery, where its branches can hang down. To keep its nice shape and dense growth, it has to be cut back by a half or one-third after flowering every two or three years. It is a native of the western and central European mountains where it grows at mountain or alpine elevations on limestone rocks and screes. In the rock garden it thrives on an acid base rock.

2

Gypsophila repens var. *fratensis* is more compact. The var. *rosea* has dark pink flowers. Larger, less dense clumps and pink-red blossoms are produced by the cultivar 'Letchworth Rose'.

Gypsophila cerastioides (2) from the Himalayas makes 2 to 4 in (5 to 10 cm) high cushions with slightly prostrate stems. The white, pink-veined flowers open in May and June. It is a lovely rock garden plant, a good grower, but only older specimens produce flowers. It should be planted in a place away from direct sun.

Gypsophila bungeana (3) is a fragile plant from Siberia and the Altai Mountains. It is about 4 in (10 cm) tall and has delicate white flowers and narrow green leaves arranged in a rosette.

1

3

Common Rock Rose
Helianthemum nummularium
Cistaceae

The helianthemums grown in the rock garden are usually named cultivars. They form large, loose clumps. In the wild, these plants mainly grow around the Mediterranean, but some species are found up to the Arctic Circle. They have leafy stems and narrow, linear-lanceolate, entire dark green leaves. The flowers are predominantly yellow, arranged in loose terminal racemes. The corolla is regular, five-petalled, the ovary matures into a capsule with three compartments (4). The flowering period is from May to September. In the rock garden, helianthemums are planted in full sun in poor, sandy, well-drained soil. They are suitable for dry walls and larger rockeries because of their robust growth. If they are to be kept in a dense, small clump, they have to be cut back considerably after flowering.

Species are propagated from seed; named cultivars are reproduced by cuttings. The seeds are sown in April, the cuttings are taken in June and kept in a cold frame or under glass. They are transplanted to their permanent place the following year.

The dry sunny slopes and the steppes of central Europe are the natural habitat of the Common Rockrose, *Helianthemum nummularium* (syn. *H. vulgare*) (1). It is a low sub-shrub with large yellow flowers.
Helianthemum alpestre (syn. *H. oelandicum* ssp. *alpestre*) (2) forms dense, low, evergreen carpets. It flowers profusely from June to August. It grows on the rocks and scree at higher elevations of European mountains, preferring a limestone substrate; it is not particular as regards soil in rock gardens.

You will more frequently encounter cultivars with single or double flowers in a wide range of colours rather than a pure species of *Helianthemum*. The species which serves as a basis for hybridization, *H. hybridum* hort., is of unknown origin. The most commonly grown cultivars are 'Gelbe Perle' — yellow, double-flowered, 'Rubin' — double-flowered, deep red (3), 'Queen' — white, single flowers, 'Supreme' — single red flowers, 'Rubens' — pink flowers with red centres, 'Rose Queen' — single pink flowers.

Helichrysum milfordiae
syn. *H. marginatum* hort.

Compositae

The genus *Helichrysum* comprises some 500 species of various shapes and sizes, including the well-known annual strawflowers with flower heads of different colours. They are distributed in Europe, Africa, New Zealand and Australia. They have undivided leaves, usually covered with felt-like hairs. The flowers are clustered in small or large multiple flower heads which are either single or in corymbous inflorescences. The fruit is an achene with a pappus (tufts of hairs which aid dispersal).

Helichrysums are cultivated in sandy soil in full sun, and require good drainage. They can be propagated by seed, although reproduction of shrubby species by half-ripe cuttings from June to August or by division in July is more common.

Helichrysum milfordiae (1), a native of Basutoland, is one of the most beautiful low-growing rock garden plants. The flowerheads have ray florets which are white inside and carmine-pink outside. Consequently the buds are pink and the open flower heads are white (2). The flowering period is from May to July. Damp is the greatest enemy of this pretty plant, and it should therefore be covered by glass in winter. If planted out in the right site, *H. milfordiae* is a rewarding plant producing an attractive, low, greyish, dense carpet and a wealth of flowers as well.

Helichrysum selago (3) is a very interesting species with decumbent to ascending, thinly branched stems. The glossy, dark green leaves densely cover the stem. They are very small, only $1/8$ in (2.5 mm) wide, and make the stem look quadrangular. The stems are terminated by small flowerheads of yellowish-white flowers. This plant should be given a place in full sun, with perfect drainage, and a topping of gravel around the base of the plant to prevent damage by damp. It is a native of the mountains of New Zealand.

Helichrysum arenarium (4) is an entirely undemanding plant. It thrives even in poor soil and, if afforded a sunny position, it attains a height of 4 in (10 cm); in a rich loam it can reach 16 in (40 cm). The single golden-yellow flower head is small but these are crowded together to make up a large inflorescence. This species flowers from July to October and requires no special treatment.

3

116

4

1

2

Hawkweed
Hieracium villosum   Compositae

There are only few hawkweeds which can be cultivated in the rock garden, despite the large number of species included in this genus. Their identification in the wild is very difficult because of the similarity of the species, the number of transitory types and the fertile hybrids. Hawkweeds are distributed in Europe and America.

They are mostly hairy or glandular, with a rosette of leaves. The terminal flower heads have only ray florets and are predominantly yellow, rarely orange to red. The fruits are cylindrical achenes each with a pappus to aid distribution.

Hawkweeds are easy to cultivate and they thrive in ordinary garden soil. Even though in the wild some species grow on limestone, they do well even in acid soil in the rock garden. However, dry, stony soil in full sun is best for them.

Propagations is by division or seed which germinates readily. Hawkweeds tend to be self-sown.

The most attractive species for rock gardens is *Hieracium villosum* (1). It is 6 to 14 in (15 to 35 cm) tall and entirely covered with dense, long, shaggy hairs, as if clothed in a light, white fur wrap. The leafy stem is occasionally branched and each branch is terminated by a single, large, bright yellow flower head measuring up to 1¼ in (3.5 cm) across. This species flowers from June to August. After some time it spreads to form large clumps. In the wild it grows on screes, rocks and high mountain plateaus.

2

118

The Mouse-ear Hawkweed, *Hieracium pilosella,* (2) is only 2 to 6 in (5 to 15 cm) high. The ground leaf rosettes send out numerous runners which make a greyish carpet. The pale, lemon-yellow flowers appear in May and often persist until October. This plant is a good lawn substitute. It is native to Europe and ranges as far as north-western Siberia.

Hieracium aurantiacum (3) is notable for the beautiful colour of its blossoms. These are deep orange to orange-red and bloom from July to August. It is 8 to 16 in (20 to 40 cm) high and native to central European mountains. Its oblong, hairy leaves are arranged in a basal rosette. It spreads profusely both by numerous offshoots and by seed, and consequently, it is not suitable for small rockeries. The hybrid *H. × rubrum* is less invasive.

Candytuft
Iberis saxatilis

Cruciferae

The genus *Iberis* comprises some 40 species distributed mainly around the Mediterranean. It includes annuals, perennials and sub-shrubs. This family is typified by flowers composed of four petals and four sepals (always two + two). The flowers are all the same size except those on the margin of the inflorescence; these florets have two much larger outer petals. These are the so-called ray florets (5).

In rock gardens, candytufts do best in full sun. They should be planted in ordinary garden soil with good drainage. It is a suitable plant for a dry wall. To preserve the nice compact shape, the plant should be cut back by a third after flowering. Candytufts are easily raised from cuttings taken from April to August. The lower trailing stems often take root, and so the easiest method is to cut off a rooted portion and plant it out.

The evergreen sub-shrub *Iberis saxatilis* (1) is only 4 to 6 in (10 to 15 cm) high. It forms dense, spherical cushions which look as if covered with snow during the flowering period from April to May. It grows naturally on rocks in southern Europe, from the Pyrenees to Sicily.

The Evergreen Candytuft, *Iberis sempervirens,* (2) has a more robust growth and attains a height of up to 16 in (40 cm). It often spreads to make large cushions, up to 3 ft (1 m) wide, and it is better suited for large rock gardens. The stems are branched and thickly covered with leaves particularly at the tips, and bearing racemes of white blossoms. When in full bloom — during May and June — the white masses of flowers completely hide the foliage. Out of flower the plant is still decorative with its glossy, dark green leaves and regular shape which is maintained by cutting back after flowering. The fruit is a rounded siliqua (3). Some attractive cultivars include the 10 in (25 cm) tall 'Snowflake', the low-growing 'Little Gem' (4) and the profusely flowering 'Nana' ('Gracilis Nana'). 'Findel' is about 8 in (20 cm) high, grows well and produces a multitude of large white flowers.

5

Iris danfordiae Iridaceae

The bulbous irises, nowadays mostly classed in the genera *Iridodic-tyum* and *Juno,* are resistant to cold but require more care than those with rootstocks. It is not always easy to prepare suitable conditions for them which correspond to those in their homeland in the Near East, i.e. ample sunshine and dry environment. They flower poorly in moist situations and are prone to diseases. Good drainage is essential, and the plants are then placed in humus-rich, sandy soil. They require plenty of warmth and a period of drought after the foliage withers. They should be planted where there is protection from heavy rain, if possible. The bulbs can be dug up when the leaves begin to turn yellow, and kept in a dry and warm place. They are replanted in October, 2$^1/_2$ to 3 in (6 to 8 cm) deep. It is advisable to feed the plant after the flowering, until the foliage withers.

Under European climatic conditions even large flowering bulbs may produce only smallish bulbils which produce no flowers. If this happens it is advisable to buy new bulbs from a reputable specialist nursery. The bulbous irises multiply by offsets and by readily germi-nating seed. The plants are able to bear flowers within three to four years.

The low-growing *Iris danfordiae* (1) has a tidy, elongated, yellowish-brown bulb coated with a fibrous skin. The flowers sometimes emerge as early as February, more often in March. The leaves begin to appear at the time of the flowering, but only after the plants have reached the final height of 12 in (30 cm). They are narrow, quadrangular, with a pale tip. After the leaves have withered, a capsule with seeds emerges above the ground.

The hardier *Iris reticulata* is more frequently cultivated. It is 4 to 6 in (10 to 15 cm) tall and produces conspicuous blue flowers in February and March. The narrow, quadrangular leaves with pale tips sometimes appear already in autumn, but reach the final height of 14 to 18 in (35 to 45 cm) after flowering. Many varieties have been bred: 'Clairette', 'Cantab' and 'Joyce' with pale blue flowers (3); 'Harmony', deep blue; 'J. S. Dijt', violet-red; (2); 'Royal Blue', dark blue, and 'Wentworth', dark violet, with central yellow stripe.

The genus *Iris* includes both low-growing and tall species as well as a number of cultivars which continue to be developed by inter-breeding. They are mostly tall plants with large flowers of various colours or colour combinations. Only the low-growing species are recommended for rock gardens. Although their flowers are smaller, they are more delicate.

These irises have a creeping tuberous rootstock and narrow or broad linear to lanceolate leaves. The large, striking flowers ripen into capsules which are ornamental in some species. The flower is regular; the three petals and three petaloid sepals are fused into a tube at the base. Three petals are larger and wider, bent outwards, and have a strip of thick, short hairs on the middle rib. The inner three are narrower and erect. The stigma is divided into three lobes con-cealing three anthers.

The rootstock irises are propagated by rootstock division, by planting the segments very shallowly (a month after flowering is the best time), or from seed sown immediately after ripening.

The low-growing — 2 to 3 in (5 to 8 cm) — species include *Iris lacustris* (1), often called *I. cristata* var. *lacustris.* This has thin, creeping rootstocks, narrow leaves and azure-blue flowers. *I. cristata* is slightly taller. These plants prefer humus-rich soil and a moist situation turned away from the sun.

Iris pumila (2) is one of the favourites. The original species has yellow or blue flowers. Hybrids of variously coloured flowers are often found in gardens.

One of the lowest-growing species — 2 to 4 in (5 to 10 cm) — is *Iris arenaria.* In April or May, the stem bears a single flower, rarely two, of rich yellow colour. The elongated, about 1 1/4 in (3.5 cm) long capsule matures in late summer (3). This species is planted in sandy-stony soil with the addition of some limestone gravel. It needs good drainage and a place in the full sun. It prefers drought in winter.

Iris graminea has narrow, grass-like, up to 16 in (40 cm) long leaves. The leaves are longer than the stalks bearing the blue flowers. The fruit is an ornamental capsule (4) with flat seeds. In the rock garden, *I. graminea* should be situated in a dry place.

3

1

2

4

Common Juniper
Juniperus communis

Cupressaceae

Junipers range in shape from slender, columnar species and cylindrical forms or spreading shrubs to low, creeping woody plants. The needles are either short, linear, prickly and more or less erect, or small and scaly. It is a dioecious plant, which means that some plants bear only female flowers and others have male flowers. The dark blue berries are used as a seasoning in certain dishes.

By combining various species and varieties of junipers, effective spots can be created in the garden. They differ both in shape and colour, including dark green, gold and silvery shades.

Junipers are light-loving plants and thrive in full sun. They thin out in shade and lose their nicely-balanced shape. They are mostly frost-resistant, only some cultivars are delicate. Junipers like a limestone substrate, but it is not essential for successful cultivation.
tion.

Rock gardens are planted with a number of varieties which are easily propagated by cuttings taken in July and August.

It is advisable to select one of the many cultivars for the alpine garden, because the species *Juniperus communis* (1) tends to look untidy. The lowest columnar juniper is *J. c.* 'Compressa' (2). It grows slowly, attaining a height of 24 to 28 in (60 to 70 cm) after many years. It has fine, 1½ to 2¾ in (4 to 7 cm) long needles. It suffers from severe frost and should be planted in a sheltered site. It can be used in a miniature rockery, planted in a trough or bowl.

Other species of large junipers also have many interesting low varieties, for instance *Juniperus chinensis* 'Plumosa Aurea' (3), which has scaly, golden-yellow leaves and attains a maximum height and width of 3 ft (1 m). It is a slow grower.

The most slender coniferous species is *Juniperus virginiana* 'Skyrocket' (4) which attains a height of 10 to 13 ft (3 to 4 m) but is only 8 to 12 in (20 to 30 cm) wide. The scaly needles (5) are silvery-grey. *J. communis* 'Stricta' with narrow, prickly needles is somewhat wider. *J. squamata* 'Blue Star' is a low-growing silvery juniper.

Lewisia cotyledon

Until recently, lewisia was an unusual plant to find in the rock garden. It is a native of California. It will thrive in cultivation only if its basic requirements are respected. Above all it needs perfect drainage to a depth of at least 20 in (50 cm). Lewisias are intolerant of too much humidity and should be planted in vertical rocky fissures, where the water can drip instead of settling in the leaf rosette. The soil has to be acid with the addition of some gravel, sharp sand and peat, and well-rotted compost or manure to ensure it is rich in nutrients. The roots near the surface are particularly susceptible to damp, and so should be topped with a layer of fine gravel to prevent rotting. The plants should never be situated in full sun and they prefer an eastern exposure. They like an occasional feed with an organic liquid fertilizer. Some species die back for the winter, others are evergreen. The evergreen species, including *Lewisia cotyledon,* should be covered with glass to be protected from winter damp. The species which die back, for example, *L. nevadensis, L. brachycalyx* and *L. rediviva,* do not need this protection.

Lewisias have long, fleshy roots and cannot be transplanted; however, they easily multiply from seed sown immediately after ripening. The seeds germinate readily and many self-sown seedlings are found in the vicinity of the withered plants. To obtain a specimen of the same colour, propagation has to be by division of the leaf rosettes. Lewisias interbreed freely, which explains the wide scope of colours.

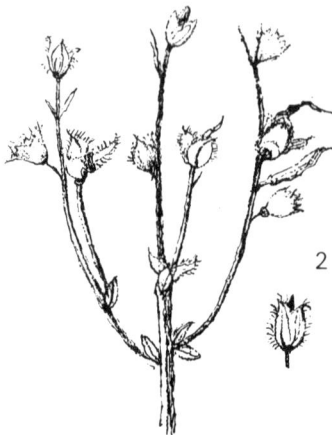

One of the most frequently cultivated species is *Lewisia cotyledon* (1). Its fleshy, smooth leaves, 1¼ to 6 in (3.5 to 15 cm) long, are often curved at the margins or red-rimmed, and so form a highly variable ground rosette. The flowers can have up to 15 petals ranging in colour from white to orange, but most often from pale pink to red and often with dark stripes. The flowering period is in May and June. The fruit is a small capsule with tiny seeds (2).

Lewisia columbiana (3) has a pale green rosette of narrow, fleshy leaves. It flowers in June and July, producing small white or pink blossoms veined with red. It is best suited to a natural rock garden.

Grape Hyacinth
Muscari botryoides
Liliaceae

Grape hyacinths are rewarding, undemanding bulbous plants, suitable for naturalizing. Their deep blue flowers are highly ornamental in spring and persist for a long time. They can be planted beneath trees, in shrub borders, or in clumps in the rock garden.

The genus comprises some 50 species distributed predominantly around the Mediterranean and reaching as far as central Europe and Asia Minor. From the greyish-white bulb grow several linear, flat or ridged leaves, and an erect stem terminated by a dense raceme of pendent flowers on short stalks. They have a bell-like corolla with six short, white lobes. The fruit is a winged, triloculate capsule.

The bulbs are planted in September and October, 2¼ to 3 in (6 to 8 cm) deep in well-drained, humus-rich garden soil. The plants die down from June to August. They are frost-resistant and can stay in the same site for years. Their bulbs are not eaten by mice, which is another advantage. They require moisture while in leaf but prefer drought conditions during dormancy. Since they are hungry plants, they should be top-dressed in autumn, preferably with well-rotted compost. Propagation is by offsets (4).

Muscari botryoides (1) is the most frequently cultivated grape hyacinth. It has two to three broadly linear, ridged erect leaves and a central flower stalk,

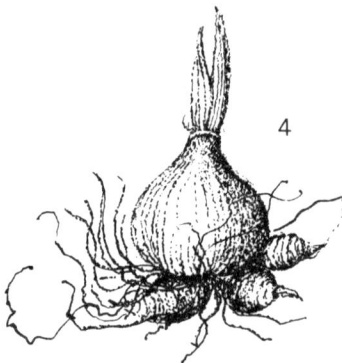

4

4 to 6 in (10 to 15 cm) tall, terminated by a dense raceme of 10 to 20 blue flowers. It blooms from April to May. After flowering, the flower stems stick out horizontally as the capsules enlarge with ripening seeds. This species is a native of southern and central Europe, where it occurs in light deciduous woodland. It is cultivated in several attractive varieties, such as var. *album* with white flowers (2) or var. *carneum* with pinkish blossoms.

The most robust species is *Muscari armeniacum*, a native of north-eastern Asia Minor. A single bulb produces six to eight narrow leaves and several 8 to 10 in (20 to 25 cm) tall stalks bearing inflorescences up to 4 in (10 cm) long. The cobalt-blue flowers last from April to May. The variety 'Blue Spike' (3) is recognizable by its large flowers.

2

3

1

Narcissus
Narcissus cyclamineus   Amaryllidaceae

Narcissi belong to the longest cultivated group of bulbous plants. The main area of their distribution is in the Mediterranean region and Europe. Gardens usually feature highly-bred large-flowered cultivars. The smaller species, however, are more suitable for the rock garden. Although the size of their flowers cannot match that of the improved varieties, they are far more delicate and charming. The leaves are linear and erect. The flowers grow either singly or in groups from the axil of a membranous sheath. The flower differs greatly according to the species or variety, but basically it always consists of a corona or trumpet varying in length, surrounded by six variously shaped perianth segments. Narcissi are divided into several groups according to the shape and size of the corona.

They require an aerated, nutrient-rich, slightly acid loam with good drainage. They like moisture in spring and dry conditions in summer. The bulbs are planted in late August and September, 2¾ to 4 in (7 to 10 cm) deep. Propagation is by offsets or by seed sown in June and July.

Species include *Narcissus cyclamineus* (1), which is only 4 to 6 in (10 to 15 cm) tall. It has a small white bulb, from which narrow leaves and a stem with a single, drooping yellow flower grow in spring. The flowering period is March or April.

It is a frost-resistant species, and the bulbs do not have to be lifted every year. In the rock garden, it is particularly effective in the company of the blue-flowered *Iris reticulata*. It is easy to cultivate. Growers have developed many attractive cultivars which often produce better flowers and are hardier than the original species.

Narcissus rupicola (2) is only 4 to 4½ in (10 to 12 cm) tall. It has narrow triangular leaves and delicate yellow flowers. It needs some protection from winter damp.

One small-sized narcissus suitable for the rock garden is the frequently cultivated *Narcissus bulbocodium* (3), the Hoop-petticoat Daffodil. It has recently been classed in the genus *Corbularia*. The small bulb (4) produces narrow leaves in autumn, and a stem 6 to 8 in (15 to 20 cm) tall with a solitary, interesting yellow flower. There are several forms of this species in cultivation.

4

1

2

3

133

Wood Sorrel
Oxalis acetosella

Oxalidaceae

There are about 800 species of *Oxalis,* but only a few are grown in rockeries and gardens. Sorrels are usually susceptible to cold, and can be cultivated only in greenhouses. They are distributed in southern Africa, South and Central America, and rarely in Europe. They are either annual or perennial, some even form small tubers. The leaves are petiolate, trifoliate or many-foliate. The flowers are regular, composed of five petals. The fruit is a capsule which forcefully ejects mature seeds over a considerable distance. The species *O. acetosella* and *O. inops* are hardy, but many of the other species come from South Africa and the tropics and so are tender in our climate. The low-growing and ornamental *O. corniculata* sometimes appears where it is not wanted. It has brownish-green leaves, yellow flowers and abundant offshoots above the ground. It can soon invade the entire rockery and has to be carefully removed.

Sorrels are propagated by seed or the bulbs around the crown of the plant.

4

Oxalis acetosella (1) is well suited for shady situations in the rock garden. Long-stalked, bright green, tripinnate leaves grow from the thin, creeping rhizome. The single fragile flowers grow in April and May on 2 to 4 in (6 to 10 cm) long peduncles. They have white petals with violet venation. In a favourable position, the Wood Sorrel forms large, weedy growths, but it can be easily restricted.

Oxalis enneaphylla (2) is more delicate but very beautiful. The tuberous rootstock sends out multiple leaves, consisting of nine to twenty two-lobed, silvery grey-green leaflets. These are followed in May and June by white to pinkish flowers. This species requires acid, humus-rich soil, good drainage and ample sunshine.

Oxalis inops (3) is completely
frost-resistant. The tripinnate leaves grow
on thin petioles from tiny tubers, and the
large, deep pink flowers have white
centres. It blooms from August to October,
doing best in full sun. It is easily increased
by its small tubers.

The smallest sorrel, Oxalis lactea (4),
also spreads readily. It has dark, brownish-
green, tripinnate leaves and dainty
white flowers.

1

3

2

Alpine Poppy
Papaver alpinum

Poppies are annual to perennial plants with variously shaped leaves. The erect stem bears a solitary, conspicuous flower. The buds hang down at first and straighten up only when they begin to open. The flowers come in various colours and sizes. Their four petals are crumpled in the bud. Two sepals fall before the flower opens. The fruit is a capsule with a number of seeds and a sessile, disc-shaped stigma.

The genus *Papaver* includes almost 100 highly variable species. Those frequently encountered in rock gardens are the low-growing, mountain *P. alpinum* and *P. pyrenaicum* which is less than 16 in (40 cm) tall. The Iceland Poppy, *P. nudicaule*, with hairy, deeply-divided leaves, forms well-developed ground rosettes. Breeding has given rise to flowers of various colours raging from white and yellow to orange and red; the true species is yellow. This rewarding plant, suitable for a larger rockery, flowers from May to autumn. It is perennial.

Poppies are propagated by seed, often by self-sowing. Older specimens cannot be transplanted because of their taproot.

Papaver alpinum is native to the European mountains, from the Alps to the Caucasus. The greyish-green leaves on long stalks are doubly or triply divided into fine segments and form an ornamental rosette, from which grows the erect, leafless stem, 4 to 6 in (10 to 15 cm) tall, terminated by a single large flower up to 2 in (5 cm) across. The elongated capsule contains a large quantity of seeds which fall out through openings underneath the stigma (3). There are two subspecies: *burseri* with large, white flowers (1) and *kerneri* with yellow to orange-yellow flowers (2). These undemanding rock garden plants, with their large decorative flowers and attractive finely-cut leaves, succeed best in rocky crevices or screes in gravelly alkaline soil and a sunny situation.

Papaver pyrenaicum is of similar appearance. The leaves are a darker shade of green and the petals are broader. *P. pyrenaicum sendtneri* has white flowers and grows on limestone rocks. *P. pyrenaicum rhaeticum* produces yellow flowers and does well on both acid and limestone substrate.

The main area of distribution of this large genus is the North American mountains. It comprises over 200 species very variable in shape, including perennial, annual, biennial plants ranging from low-growing cushion-forming species to plants attaining a height of 2 ft (60 cm). The leaves are opposite, of various shapes; the variously coloured flowers are symmetrical, with a long or short tube.

Penstemons are planted in a dry, warm, sheltered site with good drainage. They require humus-rich garden soil with added gravel and pine needles if obtainable. They can be situated in full sun as well as in a position turned away from the sun. Successful cultivation requires an acid base rock, because penstemons do not tolerate lime. Protection against winter damp is necessary for *P. caespitosus*. Penstemons often succumb to the so-called die-back, when a part of the plant withers. The affected branch should be removed and the plant cut back. It will soon produce new growth. Some creeping species spread heavily over a wide area which they can be allowed to do in a large rockery, but they must be cut back and kept under control in a smaller area.

Propagation is by taking cuttings in May or June or by seeds sown in February or March. The trailing species take root freely, and they are easily reproduced by cutting off the rooted offset.

2

Penstemon pinifolius (1) is an 8 to 12 in
(20 to 30 cm) tall sub-shrub with fine,
needle-like, evergreen leaves and bright
red tubular flowers emerging in July and
August. It is native to New Mexico and
Arizona.

3

1

The creeping species include the
beautiful *Penstemon cardwellii* (2). It has
trailing stems which root readily. In June
and July it is covered with a multitude of
flowers, often blooming again in the
autumn. It seeks humid situations in the
wild.

Penstemon hirsutus (3), also known as
P. pubescens, forms a clump about 12 to
16 in (30 to 40 cm) high. The white to
bluish-lilac flowers appear in June and
July, occasionally in August. The
profusely flowering variety 'Pygmaeus' is
only 6 in (15 cm) tall.

Moss Pink
Phlox subulata   Polemoniaceae

Some 60 species of the genus *Phlox* are distributed in North America. They include tall, medium-tall and low-growing creeping species. Many cultivars are the result of interbreeding, and they come in a wide range of colours.

The cushion-forming or carpeting species or varieties are best suited to rock gardens, particulary *Phlox subulata*. A larger rockery can accommodate *P. divaricata* which after some time makes a dense clump up to 16 in (40 cm) tall. It has large, sweet-scented pale lilac flowers.

Phlox are rewarding, profusely flowering plants. They can be situated among conifers as lawn substitutes, and they look well in borders of flowerbeds. They should be planted in moist humus-rich soil, in the sun or in light shade. Overgrown cushions are cut back by a third once in two years. The fruit is a capsule with small seeds (4).

Propagation is by division after flowering or by taking cuttings in July. Seeds are sown in early winter.

1

Phlox subulata is widely distributed and very rewarding. It spreads to form large carpets, from April to June covered with masses of flowers. Many large-flowered varieties of various shades have been cultivated, for instance the pink-purple 'Atropurpurea' (1).

Phlox douglasii is lower and more compact, forming cushions or carpets about 2 to 4 in (5 to 10 cm) high. The flowers are a pale lilac colour, purple to scarlet with dark eye, or white. The flowering period is in May and June. Some hybrids are easier to cultivate and flower more profusely, such as 'Rose Cushion' (2), suitable even for small rockeries.

North America is the home of the 6 in (15 cm) tall *Phlox amoena*. It is covered with fine down; the stems are decumbent to erect, making sparse cushions. From April to autumn, it bears masses of pink-red flowers. The garden form 'Rosea' with dark pink flowers and 'Variegata' (3) with yellow-white and pink-streaked leaves are also available. They should be planted in light shade.

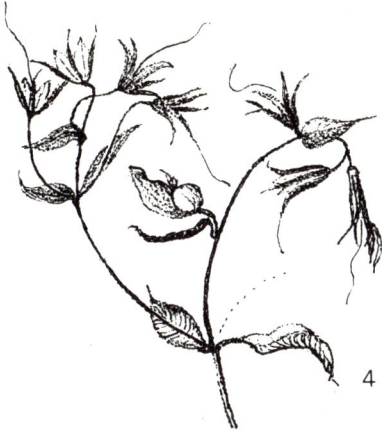

4

3

2

Hart's Tongue Fern
Phyllitis scolopendrium

Polypodiaceae

The creeping rhizome bears leathery, lanceolate, entire fronds on short, scaly stalks, with lobes at the base; these tongue-like fronds gave rise to the fern's common name. The midribs, stems and undersides of the fronds of young ferns are densely covered with rust-coloured growths. The leaves are 1½ to 2 in (4 to 5 cm) wide and reach a length of 8 to 16 in (20 to 40 cm), in favourable conditions up to 20 in (50 cm), exceptionally even more. They form a beautiful clump. The fronds are evergreen but can be damaged by frost in winter. New fronds grow in late spring and early summer.

The Hart's Tongue Fern is native to the humus-rich woodlands of Europe, Asia and North America. It also occurs in Japan. In the wild it grows in a humid microclimate on shaded rocks and in woodland screes on limestone. It should be planted in a shady position in humus-rich, alkaline soil. It does best in crevices between stones. It can be reproduced from spores but cultivated varieties rarely produce any and should be propagated vegetatively. The easiest way is by division of clumps, or by leaf cuttings in spring. The leaves are cut off with a piece of the stock, placed on moist mixture of sand and peat, and placed in a propagating case. After several months, when small buds appear, the leaves are transferred to a cooler place to acclimatize. They take at least a year to make strong plantlets.

Although the genus *Phyllitis* numbers eight species, only *P. scolopendrium* (1) is cultivated in rock gardens. Its conspicuous, deep green leaves bear sori on their undersides. There are several ornamental varieties with leaves of different shapes: for instance 'Marginatum' (2) has leaves with narrow blades and distinctly curved, almost lobed margins. In the cultivar 'Cristatum' (3) most of the blade is smooth and only the remaining third at the top of the frond is comb-like and frilled. Other interesting cultivars are: 'Capitatum', 'Conglomeratum', 'Crispum', 'Laceratum' and 'Undulatum'.

1

2

3

143

Rampion

Phyteuma comosum Campanulaceae

The new name of this plant is *Physoplexis comosa* but the older name is still commonly used in gardening. The genus *Phyteuma* numbers some 30 species. These are low to medium-tall, perennial plants with petiolate leaves arranged in a basal rosette. The leafy stems bear blue, blue-violet or whitish flowers packed in dense heads or spikes.

Some species are easy to cultivate, others have taxing requirements. *Phyteuma comosum* is the most difficult, but also one of the most sought-after rock garden plants. Its homeland is the southern region of the limestone Alps where it grows in rocky crevices on vertical walls turned away from the sun. Similar conditions have to be created in the rock garden. It should be planted in a limestone crevice, with an eastern exposure. The soil should be limy, rich in humus and with added gravel and well drained. The plant must be protected from full sun and permanent moisture, and from snails which regard it as a delicacy.

Rampions are propagated from seed sown after ripening, in August or September. The seeds germinate readily, and the plants can be transferred to the rock garden after two years.

Phyteuma comosum (1) is only 2 to 4 in (5 to 10 cm) high. The flowers are inflated below, very pale blue to white, narrowing to the tip which is shaped as a dark violet tube from which the conspicuous style protrudes. It blooms in June and July.

The habitats of the 4 to 16 in (10 to 40 cm) tall Round-headed Rampion *Phyteuma orbiculare* (2), bearing a head of dark violet flowers, are the humid meadows and rocks of Europe. It blooms from May to August, and requires humus-rich, moist soil.

The frequently cultivated *Phyteuma hemisphaericum* (3), 2 to 4 in (5 to 10 cm) tall, flowers from July to August. It is a native of Spain and the Alps. It needs lime-free, humus-rich, acid soil.

1

2

3

White Spruce
Picea glauca Pinaceae

Spruces offer some beautiful varieties suitable for rock gardens. *Picea glauca*, a native of North America, is distributed in regions with a humid climate. It is up to 80 ft (25 m) tall, but it comes in lower cultivars for rock gardens, the best-known one being 'Conica'. It does poorly in dry regions, and it is often attacked by red spider mite, which can entirely destroy even a full-grown spruce.

North American mountains are also the home of *Picea pungens*. It attains a height of 100 ft (30 m); several nice rock garden varieties have been cultivated. The Colorado Spruce has many transitory forms, covered in gardening terminology by the name *P. pungens* 'Glauca'.

The Norway Spruce, *Picea abies*, has been bred into many varieties, which are hardy, undemanding trees of various sizes. Of attractive appearance are the slow-growing 'Maxwellii' with dense, spherical growth and 'Acrocona', which spreads to form a wide growth and bears cones at an early age. 'Tabuliformis' and 'Nidiformis' are hardly 3 ft (1 m) tall, but they spread very wide. 'Pygmaea' develops numerous short twigs covered with buds, and has a spherical shape.

Varieties are propagated by cuttings in July and August. They can also be reproduced by grafting in early spring or autumn.

The most commonly cultivated spruce is *Picea glauca* 'Conica' (1) with pale green, short needles, enveloping the twigs from all sides. It has a regular conical shape, and reaches a height of 10 ft (3 m). It is densely branched and extremely slow-growing.

Picea abies 'Nidiformis' (3) forms large, flat cushions with nest-like depressions in the middle. It has short, dense, dark green needles. It is planted

1

3

only in large gardens because it can
spread to a width of up to 20 ft (6 m).
Of similar appearance is 'Tabuliformis'
but it has a flat top.

  Picea pungens 'Globosa' (2) is a dense,
flat-topped, rather spherical bush. The
short new twigs have needles of a pure
silvery shade. It will eventually grow
quite large although it is advertised as
a dwarf conifer, so this should be borne in
mind when purchasing the plant.

147

Mountain Pine
Pinus mugo
Pinaceae

Pines are represented by many beautiful varieties suited for rock gardens. The most attractive is *Pinus leucodermis* 'Pygmy', attaining a height and width of barely 20 in (50 cm) after many years. Of a similar size are the dwarf cultivars of the Scots Pine, *P. sylvestris* 'Nana' and 'Pygmaea'. The cultivar of the White Pine, *P. strobus* 'Nana', a densely-growing variable form, is slightly bigger. One of the most elegant dwarf forms is *P. sylvestris* 'Watereri' which has dense, blue-green needles. It can reach a height of 10 ft (3 m). The Mountain Pine *P. mugo* is often encountered in rock gardens.

Pines are light-loving trees, and they assume their best appearance in an open sunny situation. They are hardy and undemanding, do not suffer damage from frost and do well in poor, stony soils. Species are propagated in early spring by seed; cultivars are increased vegetatively. Because cuttings often fail to take root, grafting is often a better method. Pines with five needles in each cluster (*P. cembra, P. strobus, P. aristata, P. peuce*) are grafted on *Pinus strobus,* pines with two needles in each cluster (*P. sylvestris, P. mugo, P. nigra, P. leucodermis*) on *P. sylvestris.*

Pinus mugo (2, 4), also known under the name *P. montana,* is best suited to natural sections of the garden, because it can grow to a height of 10 to 13 ft (3 to 4 m). The plants grown from seeds will vary in their habits. Some have trailing lower branches, others ascending to erect, and the needles may be short or long.

Pinus mugo var. *pumilio* (3) reaches a height of only 3 ft (1 m). Its growth can be restricted by cutting back the new spring shoots. It grows slowly and will become very dense. Care must be taken to cut back all the shoots.

Pinus aristata (1), the Bristle-cone Pine, is the oldest known living woody plant. A native of North America, it was introduced to Europe only recently. At the tips of the shoots, the needles grow in the shape of a shaving brush. The needles remain on the branches for up to 12 years. The needles exude resin.

Pleione bulbocodioides
syn. *P. pogonioides*
Orchidaceae

The large flowers of pleiones are the true gems of our rock gardens. They are ground orchids native to Tibet, where they occur at heights from 6,000 to 10,500 ft (1,800 to 3,200 m). A proper site is the first prerequisite of successful cultivation. Pleione does best if exposed to the east or north-east, where it is affected only by the morning sun. It also requires an open, acid, slightly gravelly soil. It is advisable to plant pleiones in lime-free leafmould with the addition of some sharp sand, coarse gravel and sphagnum moss peat. Good drainage is very important. It is recommended to feed the orchids to encourage growth and to obtain a good display of flowers. Only soft water should be used, and you should mist the plants over in hot weather.

The tubers are planted in early spring in a sheltered position and a part of the tuber must protrude from the ground. The plants require protection from winter damp, so should ideally be covered.

Of all the species of *Pleione,* the easiest to cultivate is the frost-resistant *P. bulbocodioides* (1). The small, dark green tubers produce in early spring 4 in (10 cm) tall stems bearing large, carmine-pink flowers in April. The dark green leaves appear after flowering. These are about 6 in (15 cm) long and about 1½ in (3 to 4 cm) wide. They die back in October.

Pleione formosana (2) is more vigorous but is susceptible to frost. It has bigger tubers and flowers (3) and measures some 6 in (15 cm) in height. The flowers are paler, but differently coloured varieties have been cultivated, ranging from white to dark carmine-pink. This species will grow outdoors in a sheltered spot or can be grown in a cool greenhouse.

1

2

3

151

Polygonum, Knotweed
Polygonum affine
Polygonaceae

The genus *Polygonum,* represented by some 150 species, is distributed throughout the world, particularly in the temperate zones. They vary in shape and height; some are erect, others twining; some are annual, others perennial or even shrubby. There are low-growing species suitable for larger rock gardens which have erect or trailing stems and bear narrow leaves. The tiny flowers are grouped in terminal pseudo-spikes.

Polygonum affine is the most commonly cultivated species, followed by *P. vacciniifolium* and the interesting, spreading *P. capitatum* with flowers clustered in heads. All are native to the Himalayas. European mountains are the homeland of the inconspicuous *P. viviparum.*

Humid meadows in central Europe, Siberia and North America are the habitat of the taller *Polygonum bistorta* with its large spikes of deep pink flowers. It blooms from May to July, and sometimes again in August and September.

Polygonums are cultivated in moist, humus-rich soil, in the sun as well as in light shade. Those situated in the sun and in poor soil tend to be lower-growing and less spreading. Propagation is by division in early spring. The trailing stems take root easily and they can then be divided and planted.

The ornamental and undemanding *Polygonum affine* (1) has entire evergreen leaves. The stem, 6 to 10 in (15 to 25 cm) high, is terminated by a dense inflorescence composed of tiny pink flowers, which open from August to October. The plant remains decorative even after flowering, because both fruits (2) and foliage turn a rich red. In favourable conditions this species quickly forms extensive carpets.

Polygonum vacciniifolium (3) is found in the high altitudes of the Himalayas. It is a low-growing, creeping, much-branching plant, in summer covered with tiny pink flowers up to 2¼ in (6 cm) long, arranged in inflorescences. It needs to be protected from damp in winter.

Polygonum viviparum (4) is only 4 to 6 in (10 to 15 cm) high. It is a clump-forming plant with narrow, elongated, petiolate leaves arranged in a rosette, from which grow straight stems with small pink flowers held in a narrow inflorescence. It flowers from June to August. The inflorescence sometimes bears tiny bulbils in place of flowers which can be used for easy propagation.

Pink Cinquefoil
Potentilla nitida   Rosaceae

About 300 species of the genus *Potentilla* are found in the Northern Hemisphere, mainly in the temperate zone but also in the mountains. Many ornamental, low-growing or taller plants or even shrubs are cultivated in gardens. The leaves are mostly compound; the five-pe-talled flowers are yellow, white or red. A typical representative of the woody cinquefoils is *P. fruticosa* and its many profusely flowering cultivars. Low-growing subjects, such as *P. f.* var. *mandschurica* or 'Red Ace', can be grown in a small rockery. As a rule, they are unde-manding plants, making do with humus-rich garden soil and a sunny site.

A more demanding species is *Potentilla nitida,* a native of the lime-stone and dolomitic eastern and southern Alps and Apennines. It prefers a dry, south-facing, sunny site with good drainage. It should be planted in a rocky crevice or on limestone scree. If given humus-rich, sandy soil with plenty of limestone gravel, it will produce flow-ers.

Cinquefoils are propagated by division in September or by seed in February and March. Woody species are propagated by cuttings in early summer.

Potentilla nitida (1) has deep pink petals, creating a beautiful combination of colours with the silvery carpet of foliage. Unfortunately it never flowers so profusely in cultivation as in the wild.

The 2¼ to 3 in (6 to 8 cm) tall, undemanding *Potentilla ambigua* (2) is native to the Himalayas. It flowers from June to August. Planted in sandy garden soil in the sun, it spreads its trailing stems, woody in the lower part, to form large carpets. The thin rhizomes grow underneath stones, and this cinquefoil can sometimes suddenly sprout through a firm cushion of a saxifrage. The plant then has to be moved to a more suitable place where it can spread more freely.

The taller species include *Potentilla nepalensis,* a native of the Himalayas. It flowers from June to August. It thrives in any type of garden soil and tends to be self-sown. Its height is from 16 to 24 in (40 to 60 cm) which makes it unsuitable for small rock gardens, and the attractive variety 'Miss Willmott' (3) is used instead.

3

1

It is not easy to choose from the almost 600 species of primulas. They are mostly perennial, spring-flowering plants, distributed mainly in Europe and Asia with a few species coming from America. The leaves are arranged in a ground rosette and the largish flowers are solitary or arranged in various types of inflorescence. The fruit is a capsule. They include alpine species suitable for miniature gardens, such as *Primula minima* or plants growing up to 3 ft (1 m) in height like P. *florindae.*

Ornamental primulas are popular not only with private gardeners, but they also attract the attention of plant breeders and horticulturists who have developed many new forms. Some are suitable only for greenhouses, while others can be used in rock gardens.

The species are easily propagated by seed; garden forms can be increased only by division. Most species do well in humus-rich, slightly acid soil, in sun or in light shade. Their flowers last for a long time.

4

Primula minima (1), the smallest of all primulas, is native to the mountains of central and southern Europe, where it inhabits stony areas and rocky crevices on an acid base rock. It blooms in April with flowers sometimes persisting until June. It does not spread so freely in lowlands, and usually produces fewer flowers than in its natural habitat. It should be planted in a slightly acid, humus-rich soil, ideally with the addition of some moss peat and gravel. It likes moisture and must be situated in a position away from the sun, never on a southern slope.

Other alpine primulas include *Primula auricula* (2). It is found in the wild in the alpine and mountain belts on limestone rocks. It blooms from March to June. In the rock garden, it will succeed in a crevice between limestone boulders out of the sun.

Primula rosea flowers in early spring: the flowers are a glowing pink in colour. A rosette of pale green, toothed leaves is formed after flowering. The most frequently cultivated variety is the large-flowered 'Grandiflora' (3). This primula thrives in peat and bog gardens or at the margins of pools.

Primula marginata (4) is noted for its beautiful, lilac-coloured flowers and attractive leaf rosettes. It requires a light site but not in full sun.

1

2

3

Pasque Flower
Pulsatilla vulgaris
syn. Anemone pulsatilla

Ranunculaceae

Most rock gardeners keep in their collections one of the many varieties or species of *Pulsatilla*. These attractive plants are suitable for rock gardens, because they form a large clump within a few years. The leaves develop fully only after flowering. These are long-stalked, often pinnate in thin segments. The stem leaves are divided into linear, hairy segments. The flowers have six petals, hairy on the outside. The fruiting plants are also ornamental. The peduncles become markedly elongated and the maturing achenes, each with long pappus form large, feather-like spheres (4).

Pulsatillas are planted in a sunny site, in well-drained, preferably limy soil, but they also do well in an acid substrate and need no special care. Propagation is from the freely-germinating seed, sown immediately after ripening. The colour, however, cannot be guaranteed in the offspring, so if the same colour is desired, propagation must be done by division of the rhizome, but this method does not always succeed.

Pulsatilla vulgaris (1) is grown for its large flowers, which are produced in March and April. The usual colour is pale to dark shades of violet, but the improved varieties range from white to rich red and claret.

One of the loveliest species of this genus is the Spring Anemone, *Pulsatilla vernalis* (2). It has glabrous, simply pinnate, evergreen, petiolate leaves. The stem leaves are divided into linear segments and covered with rust-tinged hairs. The flowers are large, open, white inside and off-violet outside, covered with hairs. It blooms from late March to May. In the wild it can be found on grassy, sunny hills and in open pinewoods. Cultivation is rather difficult. The acid soil should be composed of rotted turf, sharp sand, with pine needles incorporated and the plant should be situated in light shade. It is propagated from seed.

The Field Anemone, *Pulsatilla pratensis* ssp. *nigricans* (3), inhabits dry, sunny slopes and stony hillsides. The flowers are considerably smaller than in *P. vernalis,* and they remain more closed. The leaves are divided into narrow segments and develop fully after flowering.

2

4

3

1

Pyrenean Primrose
Ramonda myconi
syn. *R. pyrenaica*

Gesneriaceae

The genus *Ramonda* has survived since the Tertiary Era. It has been preserved in the Pyrenees and on the Balkan Peninsula by the following three species: *R. myconi, R. nathaliae* with four to six-petalled, dark blue flowers and yellow anthers, and *R. serbica* with purple anthers. All these species have white-flowered varieties. The closely-related genera *Haberlea* and *Jankaea* have the same history and basic requirements.

In the wild, Ramondas seek rocky crevices in humid, shaded locations. They must be planted on a north-facing slope, preferably in a crevice between stones, to allow the water to drain freely instead of remaining in the rosette of leaves. The humus-rich soil should ideally be mixed from rotted turf, leafmould, peat, sharp sand and crushed rubble, with some additional sphagnum moss peat to maintain moisture around the roots.

Ramondas are propagated by seed. The seeds germinate readily, but because they are very fine, they have to be watered carefully or, better still, misted with water. An easier method, however, is by leaf cuttings. A leaf is cut off at the roots in May, the lower one third is inserted in peat in a pot and left in a shaded place. The leaf must not be removed until it has withered and new plantlets have formed. In spring, ramondas can be propagated by separation of newly-formed rosettes.

2

Ramonda myconi (1) has large rosettes of dark, evergreen, wrinkled leaves, up to 8 in (20 cm) across. The violet-blue, slightly pendent flowers appear in June and July. The corolla has four to five points; the anthers are markedly yellow.

The species of the genus *Haberlea* also form large rosettes of leaves. They usually grow in tight clumps pressed close against rocks to prevent the penetration of water. The flowers are a bluish-violet in colour; the petals are arranged symmetrically. They bloom in May and June. Two species native to Bulgaria are common in rock gardens: *H. rhodopensis* (2) has ovoid-lanceolate, sparsely hairy, roughly toothed leaves and one to five flowers borne on the stem. *H. ferdinandi-coburgi* has smallish, glabrous leaves and flowers of a more lilac colour. The requirements, cultivation and propagation are the same as for *Ramonda.*

1

Mountain Buttercup
Ranunculus alpestris
Ranunculaceae

There are about 800 species of buttercups distributed throughout the world. They are mostly perennial plants and offer a wide selection of handsome, low as well as tall-growing plants suitable for the rock garden. The flowers are usually yellow or white, have five petals and a number of stamens and ovaries; these latter contain seeds which ripen into achenes. Buttercups favour lowland plains and marshlands, but they are also found in the subalpine and alpine regions of European mountains. The high-mountain species are difficult to grow at lower altitudes. Owing to the wide distribution of this genus, the individual species differ in their cultural requirements. Propagation is by seed sown from February to April, or by root cuttings in August and September. The plants which have already formed clumps can be divided, preferably in spring.

Ranunculus alpestris (1) is a native of the high European Alps. It flowers in May and June, sometimes producing a second flush of flowers in September. The fruits are achenes with long, straight 'beaks'. In the wild it grows on both acid and calcareous rocks. Cultivation is not easy. *R. alpestris* requires good drainage, but also moist, sandy to stony, humus-rich soil. It does best in the company of other high-mountain, non-invasive species, such as *Gentiana verna* and *Cerastium alpinum.*

The Glacier Crowfoot, *Ranunculus glacialis* (2), is another tricky high-mountain species. Its petiolate, glossy, glabrous, dark green, tripinnate leaves are arranged in a rosette. The stems are 3 to 5 in (8 to 13 cm) long and carry up to three large flowers. The

sepals are covered with rust-coloured hairs. The petals are white, with a pinkish tinge on the outside and there are a number of deep yellow stamens. The achenes have a long, hooked 'beak'. Cultivation is not particularly easy. It needs neutral loamy soil with some extra peat, sharp sand and leafmould incorporated, and a sunny situation. Moisture in the soil must be maintained throughout the summer.

Another European mountain species, *Ranunculus montanus* (syn. *R. geraniifolius*) (3) is up to 8 in (20 cm) tall and produces lovely golden-yellow flowers. The calyx is covered with hairs. It blooms from May to July. It succeeds in any type of garden soil if given a sunny position.

163

Raoulia glabra

Out of some 25 species of the genus *Raoulia,* distributed in the mountains of New Zealand, Australia, New Guinea and Tasmania, only a few can be successfully grown in our gardens. The clump and cushion-forming species cannot usually be grown, while the carpeting species are more adaptable to European conditions. In their natural habitat they are confined to poor, gravelly soils, scree and plains, where they grow in full sun, mostly on granite. They should be planted in the sun, in humus-rich, gravelly, moist soil with good drainage. The stems can be surrounded with gravel to avoid excessive moisture. They will not tolerate lime; the soil must be slightly acid. All species suffer from winter damp, and thus they must be carefully covered with a pane of glass. Only *R. glabra* is relatively hardy. Raoulias are propagated during the summer by division, by cuttings taken in spring or by seed. The trailing stems take root readily and the twigs can be cut off and used for reproduction.

Raoulia glabra (1) is the most frequently cultivated rock garden species. It spreads to form low, bright green mats. Tiny flower heads cover the green foliage like white stars from June to July.

Raoulia subsericea (2) has trailing, leafy stems, and narrow, elongated, sharp-pointed leaves which form large close carpets. The small white flowers appear in June.

The smallest *Raoulia* described here, *R. lutescens* (3), is less than 1/4 in (5 mm) tall, has thin, creeping, rooting stems, bright yellow flowers in miniature flower heads, and it spreads slowly.

A silvery carpet is made by *Raoulia australis* (4). It has trailing stems and grey, broadly ovate leaves, downcurved at the tip and covered with fine hairs. The flowers are small with white ray florets and pure yellow disc florets.

1

4

3

2

Rhododendron impeditum

Rhododendrons include plants suitable from all types of rock gardens. Most species require acid soil. Only a few of them will tolerate lime, for instance *R. hirsutum* and *R.* 'Praecox'. The soil should be well aerated and rich in humus, so add plenty of leaf mould and fibrous peat. Since rhododendrons are intolerant of heavy clay soils and stagnant water, they must be provided with good drainage. Their natural habitats are in mountain areas, where they enjoy a humid climate and moist soil. In the lowlands, these requirements are substituted by planting them in the shade of trees and by frequent watering. It is important to water the evergreen species amply in dry periods and it is advisable to mulch over their roots to prevent desiccation as they are surface-rooting. The soil around the roots should not be dug but just kept free from weeds.

Botanical species can be propagated by seed sown immediately after ripening. In the low-growing species the lower branches can be layered. This consists of pegging down a branch and covering it over with soil. The branch will take root and can be detached after two years. Some species can be raised from cuttings of the current year's growth taken in July and put in a propagating frame. This method, however, often fails.

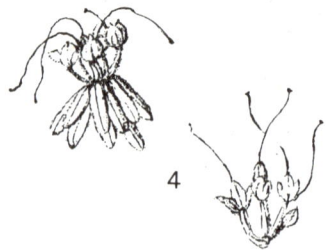

The hardy, evergreen species *Rhododendron impeditum* (1), only 12 in (30 cm) tall, can be used even for a small rockery. In April the shrub is clothed with blue-violet flowers maturing into small capsules (4). It is a native of China's high mountains.

The Alpine Rose or Alpenrose, *Rhododendron ferrugineum* (2), and the Hairy Alpine Rose, *R. hirsutum* (3), are two fine taller species. These evergreen shrubs can reach a height of 2 ft (60 cm). *R. ferrugineum* has dark green, leathery leaves, glossy above and rusty below, rolled at the edges. It flowers in June. Its native habitat includes the Alps, Apennines and the Pyrenees, where it grows in acid, humus-rich soils and peat bogs. Therefore, additional peat should be added to the soil in cultivation. *R. hirsutum* has dark green leaves with ciliated margins. Its red flowers open at about the same time as the previous species. It is a native of the Alps, where it grows on sunny slopes, mainly on calcareous substrates (an exception among rhododendrons). Both species are best propagated from seed because cuttings often fail to take root.

2

3

Reticulate Willow
Salix reticulata

Salicaceae

Willows are deciduous trees or shrubs varying greatly in shape and size. They include tall trees, shrubs of all sizes, and low, creeping woody plants, which are best suited to rock gardens. The genus includes some 350 species having the main area of distribution in the temperate and cold zones of the Northern Hemisphere. They are dioecious, i. e. the female (2) and male (3) flowers are borne on separate plants. The flowers are arranged in catkins. The fruit is a capsule containing small seeds covered with white hairs.

Willows have seeds with short-term viability, but they are easily raised from cuttings which take root readily. In creeping species, the twigs touching the ground root easily and can then be cut off and planted.

The most attractive creeping dwarf forms include *Salix reticulata* (1), which is only 2 to 4 in (5 to 10 cm) tall. The rounded leaves are dark green above and greyish-white on the underside with prominent reticulated veins. Willows flower in April, the the female catkins being much thicker than the male ones. This species is found wild in Scotland and in Europe as far north as Spitzbergen, and in North America reaches up to Labrador. It grows in grassy and stony areas, overgrown screes and rocky crevices above the tree line, predominantly on limestone. In the rock garden, it flourishes in a moist site turned away from the sun; it does well on acid rocks, too.

Another dwarf creeping willow, suited to small rockeries, is *Salix serpyllifolia* (4). It is found in the Alps on rocks, screes and in rocky crevices, usually in sunny situations. It grows above the tree line, growing on both acid and alkaline base rocks. It blooms from March to May.

4

More robust and undemanding is
Salix alpina (5), sometimes regarded as
a subspecies of *S. myrsinites*. It has
ascending branches with bright green
leaves having entire margins and
appressed hairs on the edges. It is native
to the high mountains of central and
southern Europe. It grows well in any
type of garden soil, but in the wild it
seeks limestone rocks. It has to be cut
back to prevent excessive spreading.

5

1

3 ♂

2 ♀

Soapwort
Saponaria × *olivana*

Caryophyllaceae

Soapworts are annual or perennial plants, distributed in 30 species in the Mediterranean and in central Europe. They are undemanding, do not require much care, and can remain in the same spot for many years. They do well in ordinary garden soil in a sunny situation.

Only some species are suitable for the rock gardens, one of which is *Saponaria* × *olivana*. This is a hybrid of *S. caespitosa* and *S. pumila* and is easier to grow than either of them. One of the parent plants, *S. caespitosa*, is a native of the Pyrenees. It has narrow leaves, deep pink flowers and forms dense cushions, up to 3 in (8 cm) high. The other species, *S. pumila*, is only up to 3 in (5 cm) tall. It originates from the European Alps and the Transylvanian Carpathians. It has linear leaves and large, glowing, pink-red flowers with a reddish calyx.

Soapworts can be grown from seed sown in March and April. They can also be propagated by division in July. For *Saponaria* × *olivana*, it is advisable to divide the whole clump, because by detaching only a part of it, the regular shape would be spoilt.

1

Saponaria × *olivana* (1) is very
attractive plant making dense cushions,
only 2 in (5 cm) high but sometimes up to
12 in (30 cm) across. It produces a wealth
of flowers in June. It does best in a soil to
which some leafmould and silver sand has
been added. It requires good drainage
and a sunny position.

2

The Rock Soapwort, *Saponaria
ocymoides* (2), is confined to stony
localities of south-western Europe. Its
prostrate stems form somewhat untidy
but extensive carpets, 4 to 6 in (10 to
15 cm) high. It flowers profusely in May,
June and July, producing tiny,
carmine-red blossoms. It needs a dry site
in the sun. It is suitable for dry walls or
for covering large spaces. It comes in fine
cultivars; 'Splendens' with large, pink-red
flowers, 'Rubra Compacta', with carmine
flowers, and the white-flowered
'Albiflora'.

Rockfoil, Saxifrage
Saxifraga cochlearis

Saxifragaceae

The large genus *Saxifraga* is divided into several groups. *S. cochlearis* belongs to the Silver Saxifrages or *Euaizonia,* mostly natives of the Pyrenees, Alps, Appennines and the Carpathians. They are characterized by leaves exuding lime in tiny scales on the margins, forming decorative, grey-green ground rosettes which die down after flowering. Another representative is *S. longifolia* with beautiful leaf rosettes up to 8 in (20 cm) across and with profuse flowers, or the elegant *S. cotyledon* having broadly lanceolate leaves and inflorescences up to 32 in (80 cm) tall, the only member of this group liking acid soil. Other frequently cultivated species are *S. callosa* (formerly *S. lingulata*), *S. hostii, S. aizoon* (its more recent name is *S. paniculata*) in all its forms, and other species including numerous hybrids. In the rock garden, these saxifrages do best in rocky crevices. Most species are propagated by detaching the daughter rosettes. The species without lateral rosettes are propagated from seed.

Saxifraga cochlearis (1) has small, grey-green leaves arranged in tidy rosettes forming firm, silvery cushions. It blooms in May and June.

London Pride, *Saxifraga umbrosa,* (more correctly known as *S. × urbium*) (2) from the group *Robertsonia* is a native of western Europe, the Vosges, Spain and the northern Alps. It is usually encountered in rock gardens in the variety 'Aureopunctata' with yellow-streaked leaves. The cultivar 'Elliott's Variety' makes much smaller compact mats. Both species need acid, humus-rich soil, sufficient moisture and light shade.

The annual *Saxifraga cymbalaria* (3) is 2 to 4 in (5 to 10 cm) high and belongs to the section *Cymbalaria.* It bears a mass of flowers from May to June. It is self-sown and in moist situations in humus-rich soil tends to turn into a weed, but it can be easily controlled.

3

4

2

The heavily spreading Mossy Saxifrages belong to the section *Dactyloides*. There are more hybrids than species in this section as apart from their inherent variability, they cross readily. One recently developed hybrid of *S.* × *arendsii* is 'Rosen Zwerg' (4). It is only about 2¼ in (6 cm) tall and the stem is terminated by a cluster of large, carmine flowers.

Saxifrages from the *Kabschia* (recently *Porophyllum*) group undoubt-edly rank among the most beautiful rock garden plants. They include a large number of species and many varieties. These superb plants do best in moist but very well-drained, calcareous soil. They should be planted in a mixture of loam, leafmould and sand with supplements of crushed limestone and moss peat to keep the roots moist. They do not do well in full sun and should be planted in a north- or north-west-facing situation. They flower in early spring, the buds appearing in the leaf rosettes the previous autumn. Botanical species are propagated by seed sown in February or by detaching lateral rosettes in May. The latter method is more satisfactory and the rosettes take root best in a propagating case.

One of the most beautiful species of the *Engleria* saxifrages (a subgroup of *Kabschia* section) is *Saxifraga grisebachii* (1). It is native to the limestone rocks of the Balkan Peninsula. The leaves form firm rosettes up to 3 in (8 cm) across. After flowering, the more or less abundant lateral rosettes occur around the mother plant and the cushion can then reach up to 6 in (15 cm) in diameter. The carmine-purple flowers are in fine contrast with the grey-green foliage. The stem becomes erect and elongated after flowering.

One of the best yellow-flowering hybrids is the undemanding *Saxifraga* × *boydii* (4). The tiny, grey-green leaf rosettes form thick, firm cushions. The flowers are solitary, large, held on short stems, and grow in masses.

The handsome hybrid 'Jenkinsii' (2) makes firm cushions of small leaf rosettes, and flowers profusely in March and April. The large, pale pink flowers are almost sessile at first, but later the flower stems become a little elongated.

3

The origin of some older varieties has not yet been discovered. These include 'Banshee' (3), a white-flowered hybrid which is easy to cultivate and can be recommended even to less experienced gardeners.

Two-leaved Squill
Scilla bifolia
Liliaceae

Squills are popular bulbous plants with basal, linear leaves and campanulate, usually blue flowers held in racemes. The fruit is a spherical
capsule. Over 90 species are distributed in Europe, Asia Minor,
northern and southern Africa and South America. The African and
South American species cannot be cultivated in European outdoor
conditions.

Most squills flower in the spring including *Scilla bifolia* and *S. siberica. S. pratensis* bears a dense inflorescence of tiny blue flowers in
early summer. *S. autumnalis* with three to six reddish-blue flowers is
the only species flowering in autumn.

In gardens, squills do best in humus-rich soil. They thrive both in
wooded areas and in the sun. The bulbs are entirely frost-resistant
and planted some 2¼ in (6 cm) deep in September. Propagation is by
lifting and dividing off the bulbils and by seed. The seeds have a
fleshy excrescence (caruncle), a delicacy for ants which distribute
them over long distances. Seedlings start flowering after three or four
years.

The undemanding *Scilla bifolia* (1) opens
its flowers in March and April. The bulb
usually sends out two leaves and a single
stem bearing blue flowers. The plant dies
back in June. In the wild it grows in the
Caucasus, Asia Minor and Europe, in
damp, humus-rich woodland or thickets,
and in moist meadows. It also comes in
varieties with white or pale pink flowers.

Scilla siberica (2) blooms in March and
April and has large, deep blue flowers.
Varieties with white flowers, 'Alba', or
pink flowers, 'Rosea', are also available.
The fruit is a spherical capsule (4). The
natural habitat of this species is
south-eastern Europe, Asia Minor and
central and southern USSR.

The robust Spanish Bluebell, *Scilla
hispanica,* a native of the Iberian
Peninsula, has large bulbs,
linear-lanceolate leaves, and a 12 in
(30 cm) tall stalk with a raceme of
violet-blue flowers emerging in May and
June. It flourishes in humus-rich, moist
soil in light shade. It is propagated from
bulbils. Many varieties have been
developed: 'White Triumphator' with
white flowers; 'Queen of the Pinks' and
'Rosabella' (3) with pink flowers;
'Excelsior' and 'Myosotis' with flowers
in various shades of blue.

1

2

3

4

Stonecrop
Sedum acre

Crassulaceae

Stonecrops are undemanding plants which produce masses of flowers over a long period and are easy to propagate. The flowers range from white and yellow to pink and red. The genus includes about 300 species found, with a few exceptions, in the Northern Hemisphere. They embrace species suited for both small and larger rock gardens for they vary in form and habit although most are trailing or mat forming. Stonecrops like dry conditions in full sun and require a well-drained sandy loam. After flowering, the older sedums have to be cut hard back from time to time, or replaced with newly raised plants. Propagation is simple because every small stem will take root. Some species become sprawling but can be easily checked.

One of the finest evergreen stonecrops, *Sedum acre* (1) is found on dry stony slopes, barren land, walls and railway banks throughout Great Britain and Europe and into Iran and Morocco. The bright green carpet, 2 to 4 in (5 to 10 cm) high, is covered with yellow star-like flowers in June and July.

5

4

The dry regions of Europe, including Great Britain, north Africa and Asia provide the native habitat for *Sedum album* (2) which reaches 5 to 8 in (13 to 20 cm). During July and August it is covered with small white flowers. Better suited to smaller rockeries than the species is the lower-growing *S. a.* var. *microphyllum* 'Pallens' with yellow-green leaves, and a very small rockery can be planted with 'Coral Carpet ', only 2 in (5 cm) tall, with ornamental leaves which turn red in the autumn. *S. rupestre* (3) with yellow flowers looks similar.

The Caucasus is the home of *Sedum spurium* (4). The prostrate, leafy stems tend to spread widely. The flowers occur in July in flat inflorescences. The species is available in several varieties: 'Album' with white flowers and pale green leaves, 'Ruby Mantle' with red flowers and red-brown leaves, 'Roseum' with pure pink blossoms and a few others.

Sedum spathulifolium is native to North America and Canada. The ground rosettes of succulent leaves rapidly spread to form 2 in (5 cm) high carpets. The golden-yellow flowers emerge from May to July. Acid soil is a must. This species comes in two varieties; 'Purpureum' (5) with deep purple leaves and 'Capablanca' with silvery-white foliage.

179

Cobweb Houseleek
Sempervivum arachnoideum
Crassulaceae

The most recent studies distinguish 61 botanical species of *Sempervivum;* five have been separated into the independent genus *Jovibarba*. Houseleeks are ornamental, particularly by their leaf rosettes offering a great diversity of colour and shape. The rosettes can be bright green, grey-green, brown, green, purplish or red and measure up to 8 in (20 cm) across or merely ¼ to ½ in (5 to 10 mm); some have spreading leaves, others tightly packed ones. Houseleeks are most decorative growing between stones, for instance on dry walls. A rock garden or sink planted with nothing but houseleeks can look very attractive. From the centre of the rosette grow robust, 2 to 20 in (5 to 50 cm) high flower stems. The petals are star-like; in the genus *Jovibarba* they are campanulate and pendent. The flowers are six- to many-petalled and flower from June to August. The fruit is a follicle. Many offshoots grow from the rosette producing new baby rosettes at the tips. These take root and so continue to propagate the plant. New houseleeks fill in spaces between stones or grow around and over them. These hardy plants require a situation in full sun and well-drained sandy soil. The rosette dies down after flowering, but the small lateral rosettes continue to grow.

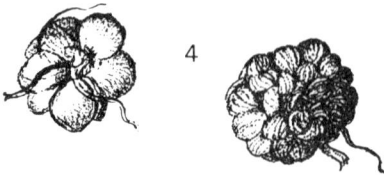

Sempervivum arachnoideum (1), 2 to 4 in (5 to 10 cm) tall, is one of the most handsome houseleeks, suited to sink gardens as well as to rockeries. It has green to brownish leaves terminated by long fibres forming a 'cobweb' on the top of the rosette. Its pink to carmine-red flowers appear in July. It is found in the wild in the Pyrenees, Alps and the Carpathians. It exists in two subspecies, several varieties and cultivars.

Sempervivum montanum (2) is also native to the Pyrenees, Alps and the Carpathians. It has dark green, pointed leaves arranged in a rosette measuring about 1 in (2.5 cm) across. From June to August it produces bright, rose-red flowers with a dark central circle.

The genus *Jovibarba* includes the yellow-flowering *J. sobolifera (Sempervivum soboliferum).* This forms numerous lateral rosettes (4) which are closed, break off easily and roll away to take root elsewhere. The flowering period is in July.

Houseleeks interbreed freely and give rise to many ornamental hybrids (3), while true species are often difficult to find.

Groundsel, Ragwort
Senecio abrotanifolius

Among some 1,300 species of *Senecio,* distributed in all continents, only a few are suitable for rock gardens. Senecios include annual as well as tree-like plants, usually tall, often straggly and not very ornamental. The few decorative species include *S. uniflorus,* a native of the Alps. It is a beautiful plant, 2 to 3½ in (5 to 9 cm) tall, greyish-white in appearance due to the covering of woolly hairs. Its leaves form a rosette and a single, large, golden-yellow flower head is produced. Cultivation has so far been rather unsuccessful. *Senecio abrotanifolius* is handsome and undemanding. Its natural distribution covers the eastern and southern Alps, the Balkans and the Carpathians. It grows on stony plateaus and screes. *S. a.* ssp. *carpaticus* grows in the Carpathians and *S. a.* ssp. *tirolensis* with orange-red flowers is found in the Alps. Senecios are propagated by seed sown in March and April, or by division of clumps in the spring or autumn.

Senecio abrotanifolius (1), 4 to 12 in (10 to 30 cm) tall, has angular stems, woody at the base, ascending to prostrate, thickly packed with leaves divided into narrow segments. The stem bears three to five glowing, orange daisy-like flower heads. It flowers from July to September.

It requires peaty, well-drained, stony soil and a sunny situation, doing well on screes where it spreads to make a sparse, dark green carpet. The trailing branches take root readily and the plant can be propagated in this manner.

Senecio incanus (2) is a difficult plant in cultivation. This native of the Alps, Apennines and the Carpathians is 2 to 6 in (5 to 15 cm) high and entirely covered with silvery felt. It has deeply lobed leaves arranged in a rosette. The smallish flowers are golden yellow and arranged in corymbs. The flowering period is during July and August, sometimes lasting until September. The cultivation of this species is not always successful. It prefers humus-rich, stony, slightly acid soil and a position out of full sun, if possible between two rocks. The similar *S. i.* ssp. *carniolicus,* a lime-loving species, is easier to grow in rock gardens.

Moss Campion, Cushion Pink
Silene acaulis
Caryophyllaceae

Campions are annual or perennial plants; a few are sub-shrubs. Many attractive rock garden plants can be found among some 400 species, such as the red-flowered *Silene schmuckeri* from Albania, 3 to 4 in (8 to 10 cm) tall, or *S. hookeri* from California, a fine, pink-flowering, delicate species.

The most typical rock garden species in the genus *Silene* is *S. acaulis*. This low-growing plant is native to the northern tundra regions and to European high mountains, where it grows on screes at subalpine to alpine levels. It likes well-drained, moist, stony, humus-rich soil and a sunny situation. It flowers profusely in the wild, the green cushions being virtually covered in pink blossoms. Although it spreads freely in gardens, the flowers are unfortunately rather sparse. Propagation is by germinating seed, division or taking cuttings.

Silene acaulis (1) is among the lowest-growing of the high-mountain plants. It forms dense, turf-like carpets, only ½ to 1 in (1 to 2.5 cm) high. The leafy stems are either flowerless or terminated by single pink blossoms which appear from June to August. It has several handsome varieties and cultivars.

The undemanding *Silene maritima*, Sea Campion, (2) originates from the coastal areas of western and northern Europe, including Great Britain. The leafy, trailing stems form relatively large, circular, grey-green cushions. It blooms from May to July. Older specimens tend to lose leaves from the centre, and need to be cut back hard after flowering to assure a nice shape for the following year. They usually start growing again the same year. The double-flowered form 'Flore Plena' has large, fragrant, white blossoms.

The profusely flowering *Silene schafta* (3), a native of the Caucasus, spreads to make sparse carpets, about 4 in (10 cm) high. It has leafy, spreading stems and pink-red flowers. The calyx is long, up to

4

1 in (2.5 cm), reddish and hairy. The fruit
is a capsule (4). This species produces
masses of flowers from June to October
and makes an attractive combination with
gentians and violets. It is very
undemanding and thrives in any type of
garden soil, in the sun or in light shade.

2

1

3

Satin Flower, Blue-eyed Grass
Sisyrinchium angustifolium   Iridaceae

Although the genus *Sisyrinchium* comprises some 70 species, only a few are encountered in rock gardens. The plants have a very short rhizome from which grow erect, narrow leaves and flowering stalks. The blue, violet-blue or yellow flowers are held in terminal spikes. The fruit is a spherical capsule.

All species are native to the temperate zone of North and South America. *Sisyrinchium angustifolium* and *S. californicum* are two species suitable for a rock garden. They are 4 to 8 in (10 to 20 cm) tall and easy to cultivate. The taller 16 to 24 in (40 to 60 cm) *S. striatum* comes from Chile and Argentina. The yellow blossoms measure 1 to 1¼ in (2.5 to 3.5 cm) and are arranged in spikes. They appear in June and July. This species is easy to grow and is particularly impressive naturalized in a part of the garden.

Some small species from the United States are well suited for rock gardens, such as *S. bellum.* This plant is easy to grow and bears violet-blue flowers from June to September.

Sisyrinchiums are propagated by sowing seed or dividing clumps. They are often self-sown, so to avoid having to weed out seedlings, cut back the stalks after flowering.

The undemanding *Sisyrinchium angustifolium* (1) is 4 to 8 in (10 to 20 cm) tall and has bright green, grass-like foliage. The stems are as tall as the leaves and bear clusters of blue flowers with yellow-orange centres which open to form an almost star-like bloom. A single blossom opens every day, fades in the evening, and another one emerges the following morning. This is a lovely plant when in full bloom in June. A white-flowered cultivar 'Album' (2) is also available. It does well in any type of garden soil, in sun and light shade. It will soon form dense clumps.

Sisyrinchium californicum (3) is a more robust species. The grass-like leaves are broader and can grow up to about 12 in (30 cm) tall, and the yellow flowers are somewhat larger. It blooms in autumn. It is only half-hardy and needs a winter protection. It flourishes in sandy, humus-rich soil in the sun.

Mountain Soldanella
Soldanella montana
Primulaceae

The genus *Soldanella* numbers only six to ten species. They are all similarly attractive in appearance and dwarf in habit. They are natives of the mountains of central Europe where they mostly grow in the high alpine regions. *S. montana* is to be found rather lower down in the forests that cling to the lower mountain slopes. This makes it one of the easiest soldanellas to cultivate.

Some species grow on acid rocks, others on limestone; this must be remembered when cultivating them in the rock garden. All require a rather shady situation and a moist but well-drained soil. Peat should be added (except for lime-loving species), to a loamy soil, together with a little gravel to ensure good drainage.

Soldanellas are propagated by seed sown as soon as it is ripe, or by division as soon as the flowering period is over.

The tender *Soldanella montana* (1) flowers in early spring. The creeping rhizome produces long-stalked, rounded or kidney-shaped glabrous leaves with shallowly notched margins. They are glossy and dark green above, reddish-brown to greenish-purple below. The stem, 4 to 8 in (10 to 20 cm) tall, is terminated by an umbel of from three to six flowers. The fragile and dainty pendent flowers are bell-shaped, fine fringed to half-way up and violet in colour. This species flowers in April. The flowering stalks become erect after flowering and the ovaries ripen into capsules containing many seeds (4).

One of the smallest soldanellas, *Soldanella pusilla* (2), a native of the Alps, Carpathians and the Balkan mountains, is only 2 to 3 in (5 to 8 cm) high and has very small, kidney-shaped or roundish dark green leaves. The delicate, lavender-coloured flowers are funnel-shaped and finely fringed at the edges. It blooms in March and April. It needs slightly acid soil with extra moss peat to keep the roots moist.

4

Of similar appearance is *Soldanella minima* (3), which is found on the high limestone Alps. It is even smaller than *S. pusilla,* only 1 to 2 in (2.5 to 5 cm) high, with white or pale violet flowers. It needs moisture and, unlike the other species described, favours a limy soil. Both *S. minima* and *S. pusilla* grow most successfully in a sink garden.

1

3

2

Yew
Taxus baccata

About seven species of yew are distributed over a large area of the Northern Hemisphere. *Taxus baccata* occurs in the lowlands and higher altitudes in Europe (including Great Britain), the Himalayas and northern Asia. It used to be common in European forests but has become much scarcer in the wild in recent years. It varies in form according to where it grows.

The Yew is an undemanding, dioecious conifer. It does well in almost any garden soil, both in full sun and shade. It has many uses in the garden: according to species or variety it can serve as a specimen plant or be planted in a large or even small rock garden. It makes a very effective hedge and grows well if kept clipped; this quality is often exploited in topiary. The dark green of a yew hedge can be used to create an impressive background to any planting. Many cultivars have been developed of various shapes and sizes with dark green or golden-yellow foliage. The low-growing ones include 'Amersfoort', 'Cavendishii', 'Standishii', 'Semperaurea', 'Repandens'; some can even be grown in small rockeries.

Yews can be propagated by seed, and the cultivars from cuttings taken in August and raised in a propagating frame shaded from the sun.

The dark green needles of yews (1) are brightened in the autumn by fleshy red arils (2) which cover the seeds. With the exception of these arils, all the other parts of the tree are poisonous.

An interesting cultivar, suited for a small rockery, is *Taxus baccata* 'Adpressa Variegata' (3). It is low- and slow-growing. Its needles are shorter than those of the species. They are a golden-yellow colour when young but later turn yellow and then green. It needs good light.

One of the loveliest golden yews is *Taxus baccata* 'Fastigiata Aurea' (4). It does not take up too much space because of its narrow, columnar habit. Although it is a slow grower, care should be taken before placing it, because it can eventually reach a height of 16 ft (5 m). It requires a protected site. It should also be remembered that its striking yellow colour must harmonize with the surroundings; this word of warning goes for all golden conifers.

American Arborvitae
Thuja occidentalis

Cupressaceae

The American Arborvitae is a frequently cultivated coniferous tree native to North America. It has scale-like needles which turn a bronze shade in the winter. The cones (4) are about ½ in (1 cm) long and these start forming only when the tree is 30 to 40 years old. This tall, columnar to conical tree is not suitable for rock gardens, but can be effectively used in hedgerows, especially in the cultivar 'Malonyana' which is tolerant of clipping.

This species is the hardiest of all arborvitae, and very undemanding. It can withstand both sun and light shade, and it is not very demanding as regards soil, although it succeeds best in a cool, moist clay soil. It tends to wither in a dry site and the needles become rather sparse in a deeply shaded situation.

Only slow-growing compact cultivars are planted in rock gardens. They are propagated by cuttings taken in August and September. Some cultivars fail to make roots and have to be propagated by grafting, preferably on the stock of *Thuja occidentalis*.

There is a wide assortment of small, slow-growing cultivars of *Thuja occidentalis* (1), such as 'Hetz Midget' or 'Ceaspitosa' which are among the smallest and, therefore, most suitable for

5

the rock garden. The cultivar 'Danica' is most attractive; a little over 20 in (50 cm) high, it forms a globular bush. 'Recurva Nana' and the beautiful, dark green 'Holmstrup' attain a height of 6 ft (2 m). 'Umbraculifera' (5) is a very dense and slow-growing cultivar, spreading to form a wide-reaching growth instead of stretching up. A spacious rock garden can accommodate the dark green, spherical 'Woodwardii' or 'Reingold', which is striking by its golden-yellow leaves turning bronze in the winter. It can grow up to 13 ft (4 m) high. Other small species include the cultivars 'Globosa', 'Little Gem', 'Spiralis', or the more delicate *T. orientalis* 'Aurea Rogersii'.

The interesting cultivar *Thuja occidentalis* 'Späthii' (syn. 'Ohlendorfii') makes a shrub and grows slowly. The ends of the long, thin branches have scale-like needles (2), the lower part of the plant bears coniferous needles (3), which are dark green with a bronze to brown-reddish sheen.

Wild Thyme
Thymus serpyllum Labiatae

The Wild Thyme does not need a detailed description as it is such a well-known plant. It grows in the wild on sloping ground on heaths, roadsides or other dry situations of Europe and Great Britain. It is highly aromatic and in summer the air is saturated with its pleasant scent. The Wild Thyme has wide usage in the garden. It flowers best in full sun, in loose, poor sandy soil. It can be successfully cultivated on dry walls, between paving or in the heath garden. The creeping stems are slightly woody and root quite easily so that the plants, in time, cover a considerable area. It should not be restricted too much, because a carpet of the Wild Thyme in full bloom is a beautiful sight. Propagation is by division or by taking cuttings.

Thymus serpyllum (1), a carpeting plant growing to a height of 1 to 2 in (2.5 to 5 cm), is found in dry localities throughout Great Britain and Europe, extending far to the north. It flowers profusely and persistently from June to September. A number of other low-growing species of thyme are often treated as varieties of *T. serpyllum*. Several coloured forms have been developed, such as the white-flowered 'Alba' (2), 'Splendens' with carmine-red flowers, 'Coccineus' with red flowers, and others. These varieties can be combined to achieve an impressive colour effect.

By crossing the species *Thymus pulegioides* and *T. vulgaris* (Garden Thyme), a handsome hybrid *T.* × *citriodorus* was formed. It is a 4 to 6 in (10 to 15 cm) tall shrub having a pleasant lemon-like odour. It has small, ovate to rounded leaves and pale pink flowers opening from May to July. The older plants have to be cut back from time to time to keep the shrubs dense and tidy. The cultivar 'Silver Queen' ('Argenteus') has white-edged leaves and 'Aureus' (3) has golden foliage.

4

The interesting species *T. doerfleri*
(*T. hirsutus* 'Doerfleri') (4) from the
Balkans is less commonly cultivated. It is
a carpeting plant covered with grey hairs,
and has narrow hairy leaves all turned in
one direction, which makes the plant look
as if it has been constantly windswept.
The pale pink flowers open in June and
July.

2

3

1

Globe Flower
Trollius pumilus

Ranunculaceae

The genus embraces some 30 species of perennial plants distributed mostly in the Northern Hemisphere from temperate to cold zones. They vary in height but all have deeply-divided palmate leaves. The little-branched, erect stems are terminated by a single flower containing a number of stamens. The petals are in fact colourful, usually yellow sepals, the petals proper being reduced to nectar-producing receptacles (4).

The most common garden species are *Trollius pumilus, T. acaulis* and *T. europaeus.* In the wild the Globe Flower grows in moist meadows, usually at higher elevations. It is advisable to place it in the rock garden in humus-rich, moist soil in the sun or light shade, for instance near the pool, where it will form beautiful, profusely flowering clumps — dry, arid sites in full sun are not suitable.

Many cultivars with striking large flowers of various colours have been developed. They are sold as *T.* × *cultorum* and include 'Canary Bird' with yellow flowers, 'Alabaster' with pale primrose yellow flowers, the orange-yellow, large-flowered 'Goldquelle', the bold deep orange 'Fireglobe' or 'Orange Princess' with large, bright orange flowers. One of the largest species, almost 3 ft (1 m) high, is 'Prichard's Giant' with orange flowers.

Propagation is by division in September or by seed.

Trollius pumilus (1), suitable even for small rockeries, is a clump-forming plant. It is 6 to 12 in (15 to 30 cm) high with dark green, long-stalked, sharply-toothed leaves divided into five palmate segments. From the centre of the leaf rosette grow numerous, usually unbranched stems, terminated by a single, large, golden-yellow flower, resembling a large buttercup. Flowering takes place in June and July. The fruits are follicles containing tiny seeds in globular heads (3). *T. acaulis* is similar and attains a height of 3 to 12 in (8 to 30 cm), *Trollius europaeus* (2) grows up to 20 in (50 cm) high and inhabits moist meadows in central Europe and Great Britain. The leaves are three- to five-pinnate; the basal leaflets are held on leaf stalks, the upper ones are sessile. The flowers measure up to $1\frac{1}{4}$ in (3.5 cm) across and are composed of a large number of spherically arranged golden-yellow petaloid sepals. The flowering period is from June to August.

2

1

Eastern Hemlock
Tsuga canadensis   Pinaceae

Tsuga is a genus of conifers containing about 15 species which are
distributed through North America and eastern Asia. *T. canadensis* is
native to eastern North America, where it grows on north-facing,
rocky slopes. It is a handsome conifer but unsuitable for rock gardens.
It can be used as a solitary plant but only in a very large garden.
There are many beautiful dwarf cultivars, however, some suited even
to small rockeries, such as 'Minuta', a slow grower, 1/2 in (1 cm) per
year, with slender needles. Other slow-growing cultivars include
'Compacta', a dwarf bush, 'Microphylla' with very small needles and
'Cole', a very slow-growing prostrate form. 'Compacta' is conical in
shape and has dense branches with small needles. An effective solitary plant in a spacious rock garden is 'Pendula', a decorative, wide
shrub with spreading to pendent branches.

Tsuga is an undemanding and hardy conifer. It flourishes in humus-
rich, moist soil in an open, light situation, but it will tolerate shade. It
suffers in dry situations. Since it is tolerant of clipping, it can be used
as a hedgerow plant.

The species can be propagated by seed (3). Cultivars are raised
from cuttings taken in autumn. They can also be grafted on *Tsuga
canadensis.*

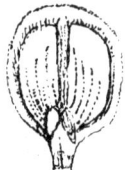

3

Tsuga canadensis has dark green
(grey-green on the underside),
comparatively short needles, about 1/2 in
(1 cm) long. The new shoots have bright
to pale green needles. The mature tree is
pyramidal in shape. The cones (1) are up
to 1 in (2.5 cm) long, ovate, pendulous and
persistent. The tree is fertile only when it
reaches an age of about 30 years.
Recent years have brought an
improvement in the range of dwarf
cultivars, growing up to 3 ft (1 m), of this
attractive woody plant. One of the
best-known is 'Jeddeloh' (2), which has
an interesting, unusual shape; the
branches bend down to the ground on all
sides from the centre of the shrub. It
reaches a maximum height of around 16
in (40 cm).

Tulip
Tulipa tarda
Liliaceae

Tulips are divided into several sub-genera and groups. Most species are found in the Near East and several in the Mediterranean, where extreme seasonal climatic conditions prevail. They are resistant to frost, but some are averse to cold, wet summers. The bulb (3) is annual, which means that the plant exhausts the store of nutrients every year and has to form a new bulb for the following year. The bulb has a prominent point and a base from which grow tight, concentric layers of modified leaves serving as a food store protected by a brown covering or tunic. The stem and foliage grow from the bulb; some species have broad, bright green leaves, whereas others are grey-green; some leaves are narrow or are marked with narrow stripes. Some tulips have their foliage arranged in rosettes, with smooth or undulating margins, sometimes with a red edge. Tulip flowers also come in a wide range of colours and shapes as several thousand cultivars have been developed. Rock gardens, however, are best planted with species that are daintier and lower growing than most cultivars.

The bulbs are often attacked by fungus or virus diseases. These are usually carried by aphids, so at the first sign of these aphids it would be advisable to spray, althought this will not be necessary with the early-flowering varieties. When a tulip develops twisted leaves, the bulb must be dug out and burnt.

The popular *Tulipa tarda* (1), only 3 to 6 in (8 to 15 cm) tall, is a native of Turkestan. It has narrow, greyish-green leaves and short, branched stems carrying one to six flowers. The flowers open to form stars with white points and yellow centres. The flowering period is in April and May. The fruit is a trilocular capsule. This species does well in any type of garden soil, both in the sun and in light shade, and soon spreads to form attractive clumps. It can remain in one spot for several years. *T. urumiensis* from Iran is very similar and has bright yellow flowers.

Another pretty low tulip is *Tulipa aucheriana* (2), native to Syria and Iran. The brown coating of the bulb is covered with fine hairs on the inner side. The leaves are linear. The plant is 3 to 4 in (8 to 10 cm) high and bears between one and three flowers on one stem. The buds are drooping but straighten up later and open into pink, starry flowers which appear in April and May.

3

Valerian
Valeriana supina

Valerianaceae

The genus *Valeriana* ranges throughout Europe, Asia, South and North America. It includes very dwarf plants (for instance *V. supina* and *V. × suendermannii*), medium-high species like *V. montana* and plants surpassing 3 ft (1 m) in height, *V. officinalis* and *V. pyrenaica,* and others, not suited for rock gardens. The scent of valerians attracts cats. Valerians are cultivated in humus-rich, moist soil near water, or in the wooded parts. Some species spread readily by means of off-shoots.

Valerians are easily propagated by division. The species form abundant underground shoots which spread freely and often become very invasive. However, they do look most attractive when massed in full bloom.

The small carpeting species *Valeriana supina* (1) is native to the eastern limestone Alps. It has small oval leaves arranged in a rosette, and erect stems with several opposite leaves. The small pink flowers form a dense inflorescence. Flowering occurs from June to August. The fruit is an achene with a pappus of hairs (5). This modest plant likes lime but does well in any garden soil. It is about 3 in (8 cm) tall, forming bright green cushions which become pink during the flowering period. It grows both in the sun and in light shade, but it tends to be lower and more compact in a sunny site. When setting valerians out, their spreading habit must be taken into account.

Valeriana tripteris (2) is somewhat taller. The stems, growing from branched rhizomes, are 4 to 16 in (10 to 40 cm) tall and bear several pairs of opposite leaves. The basal leaves are long, petiolate, and roughly toothed. The stem leaves are divided into three segments and have a toothed margin. The large inflorescence is composed of pale pink flowers lasting from May to July. This species inhabits the humus-rich woodlands of central and southern Europe in the wild. It does not form offshoots.

1

Valeriana montana (3) is a robust plant attaining a height of about 6 in (15 cm). The flowers (4) are small but form large inflorescences. In the wild it frequents light woodland and shrubby sloping ground on mountainsides.

5

3

2

4

Speedwell
Veronica filiformis

Scrophulariaceae

Some 150 species of the genus *Veronica* have been found in the cooler regions of most of the world. They include low, carpeting species, taller species reaching up to 6 ft (2 m), annuals, perennials and subshrubs. They are mostly undemanding and flower profusely. The flowers (5) are symmetrical and always have two stamens. They either grow singly in the axils of leaves, or in dense terminal racemes. They are usually blue in colour. The fruits are capsules with a notch which varies in depth according to species (6).

Veronicas are cultivated in ordinary garden soil in a sunny position. The smaller species are suitable for planting in rock gardens and on dry walls; the larger species look best in naturalized sections of the garden, in flower beds or in company with bulbous plants. Propagation is usually by division in spring before flowering or in the autumn. They can also be raised from cuttings taken in July or August.

Veronica filiformis (1) is only 1 to 2 in (2.5 to 5 cm) tall and has long, thin, prostrate stems covered with pale green, rounded leaves. The blue flowers with darker venation grow singly on long stems which arise in the axils of leaves. Flowering is from April to July. The trailing stems root readily and so the plants soon spread, particularly in moist situations, to form large, pale green carpets.

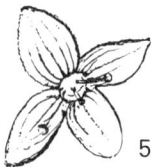

The pink-flowered *Veronica surculosa* (2) is 1½ to 2 in (4 to 5 cm) tall and completely covered in grey hairs. The trailing, thickly-leaved stems form beautiful, grey-green carpets. It flowers from May to July. It does best in a dry spot in full sun.

The low, undemanding *Veronica prostrata* (syn. *V. rupestris*) (3) has decumbent stems and abundant, dense racemes of bright blue flowers in May to July. It comes in cultivars: 'Alba' with white flowers, 'Rosa' with pink flowers and 'Spode Blue' with blue flowers.

The taller species include *Veronica incana* (4). It is 8 to 20 in (20 to 50 cm) tall and covered in grey felt. It has an erect, strong stem and lanceolate, finely toothed leaves, and forms an attractive growth even in the non-flowering period. The stems are terminated by dense spikes, up to 1 ft (30 cm) long, composed of dark blue flowers. The flowering period is in June and August.

5   6

1

2

3

4

Yellow Wood Violet
Viola biflora

Violaceae

The genus *Viola* comprises many species (up to 400 are classified), mostly of low-growing habit, distributed throughout the world. They are usually undemanding, profusely flowering and often fragrant. The variously coloured flowers are symmetrical; the lower petals have spurs. They do well in sun or shade. Propagation is by seed, division or cuttings. The fruit is a capsule (5). The seeds have a fleshy excrescence known as a caruncle. This is a favourite delicacy of ants which help distribute the plants by carrying the seeds away from the parent plant.

Violets interbreed easily and this quality made them popular with growers. The best-known hybrids are crossed with *Viola cornuta*, the Horned Violet, and the large-flowered, colourful cultivars are often available under this name. Rock gardeners should concentrate on the daintier species such as *V. biflora, V. lutea* or *V. odorata.*

Viola biflora (1) is an interesting violet from the high mountains of Europe, Asia and North America. From the creeping rhizome grow reniform-cordate, serrate, long-stemmed leaves. The erect stalks bear one to three bright yellow, nodding flowers with fine dark red lines on the lower petal which has a small spur.

Flowering occurs during May. The native habitats of the Yellow Wood Violet are rocky crevices, mountain forests and wet meadows. It prefers acid base rocks to those of limestone. It should be cultivated in moist, humus-rich soil, in light shade.

Viola lutea (2) is 4 to 8 in (10 to 20 cm) tall. It has erect or ascending stems and yellow or violet-tinged flowers, about 1¼ (3.5 cm) long. There is a dark pattern on the lower petal. It produces masses of fragrant flowers in June and July. It is native to Europe, including Great Britain.

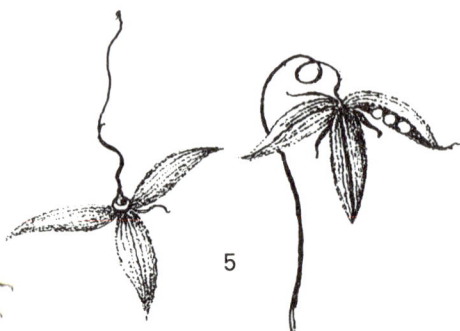

3

5

One of the best-known spring-flowering plants is the Sweet Violet, *V. odorata* (3). The petals are violet with a white base and a longish spur. It flowers in March and April, and usually blooms a second time in August and September. It tends to be self-sown. The double-flowered form is cultivated, as well as many different coloured cultivars.

The similar *Viola palustris* (4) has pale to violet, odourless flowers. It inhabits moist, peaty soils in Europe (including Great Britain), Asia and North America.

2

1

4

SOME FACTS ABOUT ECOLOGY

When setting out the plants, we should bear in mind that they are living organisms needing various requirements from their environment. Therefore try to give them conditions as near as possible to those of their natural habitat. This will often be difficult and sometimes even impossible.

Not all alpine plants are native to mountain areas. Some species originate from rocky plateaus, others from sandy or humid sites, bog or marshland, and others are found in the tundra, in the arctic regions or in high deserts. Their requirements are extremely different and you will face the challenge of re-creating as far as possible the natural habitats for your plants in the restricted area of the rock garden.

Plants are affected by a number of factors such as the intensity of the solar radiation, the regional climate and the microclimate, the humidity and the chemical composition of soil. Some of these requirements can be met, others will be difficult to provide. It is not easy to create natural conditions in a rock garden situated at an altitude of 200 ft (61 m) above sea level for a plant naturally occurring at a height of 6,570 ft (2,000 m). The plant will either die, or a low-growing, delicate specimen will grow to make an ungainly sprawling clump. It is best to give up such demanding species. However, not all plants are so conservative and unadaptable. When given adequate care, many will thrive and flower in our climate.

Mountain plants found above the tree line grow in full sun, but they do poorly in rock gardens situated in low-lying regions mainly because of the drought but also the heat. Water is one of the vital factors. If you ensure your alpine plants to get enough underground water for their roots, you can situate them in a sunny spot. Otherwise they prefer a partially shaded site, or the dappled shade provided by a tree with a light canopy of leaves. Many plants seek shady sites because of moisture and not to avoid the sun.

Although the chemical and physical composition of soil is very important, the relevance of acidity or alkalinity (the pH factor) is often overestimated. Only some species are dependent on this factor which is of no importance for others, particularly when the rest of the conditions are favourable.

In the mountains, covered throughout the winter by a thick layer of snow, the plants survive as if by snuggling under a blanket at a temperature of about 0° C (32° F). Snow is often scarce in the lowlands where severe frost can damage alpine plants. The snow cover is substituted by a covering made of dried bracken or preferably of beech leaves. Only the plants inhabiting rocky crevices in the mountains, where they are exposed to cold winds without the benefit of snow, withstand freezing temperatures. A plant cannot receive water colder than 4° C (39° F), and often remains dry in its natural habitat over winter. Some high-mountain plants suffer in our rainy winters. These must be protected by glass panes or cloches.

Spring in the mountains comes suddenly and relatively late, when the sun is quite warm and the thaw brings plenty of water. In the rock garden, the plants need to be protected from the damp and rain of winter. See each plant has a generous amount of gravel around its stem and under its leaves. Warm and cold to freezing periods follow each other in this country during winter and early spring, which can prove harmful to alpine plants and to some bulbous plants. They tend to shoot during a warm period and then succumb to frost. It is advisable not to remove any winter protection too early in order to moderate these sharp temperature changes. The same situation occurs in the autumn. If the plants are covered too soon, the combination of warm days and the covering can cause them to shoot, and the young growth will then be damaged by frost. In the autumn, the plants should be covered later rather than too early.

Many gardeners grow bulbous plants native to the deserts of Central Asia. In their homeland, these plants produce a profusion of beautiful flowers after the spring floods. The scorching sun soon absorbs every drop of water, and the underground organs (bulbs and tubers) mature in the hot sand. These plants should ideally enjoy drought and warmth in the rock garden. However, because our summers tend to be rainy, it is advisable to lift the bulbs and dry them off in a warm place until the planting time in autumn, to assure flowering in the next season.

MAINTENANCE AND CARE

If you want to enjoy your rock garden, you have to look after it with great care. It is not enough just to build it, but you must also regularly do the weeding, cleaning of leaves, watering, as well as transplanting any specimens from unsuitable sites. Some species spread fast and will have to be restricted in their growth. Others must be tended carefully and attentively because they take time to establish themselves. The time and work spent on the rock garden will be well rewarded by its beauty when it attains maturity.

Spring and autumn are of course the busiest seasons. In spring, the rock garden has to be cleared of any débris, any winter protection is removed, and the damage wrought by moles, mice or other garden pests throughout winter has to be remedied. Stones loosened by frost are set back in position and the surrounding soil is firmed down, and some more is added if necessary. Name labels loosened by frost are repaired and reinserted. Weed seedlings that have germinated or survived the harsh winter must be removed. One of the rock gardener's main worries is moss which establishes itself over the shaded and humid parts. Weeding is less urgent in summer, but you will be busy watering unless you have an automatic system and just need to turn on the tap. The summer months can be used to examine the plants to check for any signs of pests, diseases or any other disorder. Frequent inspections are advisable, and every symptom must be treated immediately, or else the trouble will spread.

Autumn is the time to plant new bulbs and get the rock garden ready for winter. Cut off any withered stems and lift bulbs and tubers of those species which will not survive the winter. Top dress the roots of rhododendrons with coarse pine needles or peat and water the plants thoroughly, if necessary. Tie up ornamental grasses and conifers to prevent their being broken by snow and to make them look tidier. The more delicate species are covered with bracken, prunings or beech leaves and fastened over with chicken wire so as not to be swept away by the wind. Plants susceptible to winter damp are covered with a pane of glass. If you have a small pool with no outlet, cover it and put a bunch of twigs, a log or washing-up liquid container in the water, otherwise the ice might damage the edges of the pool, especially if it is made of concrete. If fish are left in the pool over winter, make sure they get enough air. The best way of achieving this is to install a small pool heater in frosty weather to keep an area free from ice.

PATHS AND STEPS

All sections of the rock garden must be accessible not just to enable you to admire the beauty of the plants at close quarters, but also because you have to maintain the garden and set out new plants. You can build paths and steps in a spacious rock garden. Concrete or sandy paths would be unsuitable in a natural-style rock garden, where they should be made of the same natural stone. Choose large, flat slabs and bed them in sand to make them firm. Natural stones should be also used for steps. The paths should never be straight but meander between the rocks. Think carefully before building steps; they should lead to interesting and attractive parts of the garden as well as being a charming feature in their own right. If the garden is large you can place a simple seat or a large stone in an appropriate position.

The paths and steps look best if softened by vegetation growing between cracks and spilling over the edges. To achieve this effect choose species which will tolerate wear especially when planted between stepping stones; subjects like *Sagina procumbens, Saxifraga hypnoides* or *Thymus serpyllum* would be suitable. Such paths produce an interesting colourful effect and harmonize with the rest of the rock garden.

WATER IN THE ROCK GARDEN

Both in the wild and in the rock garden, water is always a refreshing element having, moreover, a vital ecological significance. Unless you are lucky to have a brook passing through your garden, you will have to find another way to introduce water. Then dig out a meandering bed for the water feature. It can be embellished by waterfalls, cascades and overflows tumbling into a pool or just be a straightforward pond. If you wish so you could make shallow depressions in some places around the edges to serve as waterbaths for birds. Line the bed of the depression with stretchable pool liner or a glass-fibre preformed cascade and pool to prevent leakage and add a few stones if you wish. Water in the rock garden is pleasant both to look at and for its sound. You can let the cascade to overflow into the pool and arrange the height of the lip from which the water falls so that it makes a tinkling sound.

In a rock garden it is best to use an irregular-shaped pool with the edges concealed by stones and small plants. It is possible to turn a part of the pool into a bog or marsh garden. Irregularity can be enhanced by a boulder partly submerged in the water. A perfect round or oval pool would look too artificial and spoil the natural effect. There are several ways to make the pool. The quickest and most effective method is to use black stretchable pool liner. Simply

Fig. 2. A pool with plants makes an attractive feature in a rock garden.

Fig. 3. A polythene pool is easy to make.

excavate the area to the required shape. The depth depends on the type of plants: large water lilies need a depth of at least 28 in (70 cm), medium-sized species need 12 to 16 in (30 to 40 cm) and small water lilies, like *Nymphaea pygmaea,* will grow in a depth of 6 to 8 in (15 to 20 cm). Remember that a single water lily needs at least one square yard (square metre), or else its leaves will soon cover the entire surface of the water. Other plants, such as members of the genera *Typha* (Reedmace), *Scirpus* (Bulrush) and *Butomus* (Flowering Rush), are best in a depth of 4 in (10 cm). In a bigger pool you can also shape the bottom. If you make the centre deeper than the edges by creating a marginal shelf you can plant a wider range of species.

Once the excavation has been completed make sure that the sides are as smooth as possible to prevent the sheeting from being pierced or torn by sharp stones. Bang the sides smooth with the back of a spade or preferably line the hole with a layer of damp sand. Fill the pool with water right away to make it fit firmly against the walls. The borders of the future pond should be lower than the surrounding ground. These can be covered with large stones, some of which could emerge from water and the majority should conceal the edges of the pool and the pool liner. You can use pebbles in some places. Gaps between the stones are filled with soil and a few easy-growing plants can be allowed to spread to cover any possible defects. The best plants for this purpose are Creeping Jenny, *Lysimachia nummularia,* or *Heliosperma alpina.*

Never put sharp objects in the pool when a stretchable pool liner has been used and be careful when placing the receptacles containing water lilies or other plants on the bottom. It is advisable to plant in the special plastic basket-like containers as not only is it easier to move the plants around but it keeps the soil off the floor of the pond

213

and it is easy to see if roots stray. The alternative is to plant them in soil laid over the bottom of the pool. This has several serious drawbacks. The soil will be churned by fish resulting in permanently muddy water and, in time, the whole water feature will become a tangled mass of strong-growing reeds which will have overgrown the more delicate plants.

THE BOG GARDEN, ALPINE MEADOW AND SCREE BED

The range of plants grown can be greatly increased by creating a number of specialized habitats such as the alpine meadow, scree bed, or bog garden. These features do not necessarily have to be very large and can either be constructed close to the rock garden, perhaps to get the best effect, or in another part of the garden. The bog should be built by the pool, if you have one, to which it is ecologically linked. While building the pool, a shallow area can be reserved at the margin. If a separate bog is to be built, excavate a shallow hollow, line it with pool liner if the soil is normally well drained and cover with soil. Alternatively use a naturally damp part of the garden provided it is moist throughout the year. Without fairly constant seepage of water the bog tends to dry up and a constant fresh water supply is necessary for the plants to survive. A stagnant patch is not good enough.

An alpine meadow can be situated in any part of the rock garden, both on flat and sloping ground. The choice of plants depends on its size and position.

There is a wide assortment of plants suitable for growing in the alpine meadow. Grasses are the basic ones but they must be chosen carefully, otherwise they might invade the whole rock garden. Some attractive subjects are *Festuca supina, F. glacialis* and *F. vivipara*. Low-growing sedges such as *Carex firma, C. humilis* or *C. montana* are also effective. Flowering plants are especially impressive among the grasses. The selection of species depends on the position of the alpine meadow. Low-growing plants such as gentians (*Gentiana acaulis* or *G. verna* are particularly suitable) are placed in the top sections together with some bulbous plants, like species daffodils or low-growing dainty cultivars, and various species of crocuses. A damper alpine meadow such as one situated at the foot of the rockery can feature the delightful, decorative *Anemone narcissiflora* or the European Globe Flower (*Trollius europaeus*). Bulbous and tuberous plants which thrive in a more moist environment include *Gladiolus palustris* and *G. imbricatus, Fritillaria meleagris, Narcissus pseudo-narcissus* and various species of orchids.

A scree bed is an ideal habitat for many other plants. Natural screes are formed by disintegrated rocks and accumulate in conical heaps on the lower slopes of mountains. In the garden, the scree can be transformed into a flat raised bed. Good drainage is essential. Start with a thick layer of stones or rubble, cover it with a 4-in (10-cm) layer of rich loamy compost with plenty of leafmould and slow-release fertilizer from which the plants will draw nutrients. Finally top this with a layer of coarse gravel. The scree bed is excellent for growing species with fine roots such as the Alpine Poppy (*Papaver alpinum*), Penny Cress (*Thlaspi stylosum*), Sun Rose (*Helianthemum alpestre*), *Saxifraga oppositifolia* and many others.

THE SINK GARDEN

Even those who do not have a rock garden can enjoy some alpine plants at home. A miniature rock garden can be built in an old sink, trough or other ceramic container. The size depends on the position; the usual sized sink garden can be accommodated on a patio or terrace, a miniature rock garden in a smaller container can be placed on a windowsill or balcony.

Fig. 4. A miniature rock garden in a sink or trough is a good idea if space is at a premium.

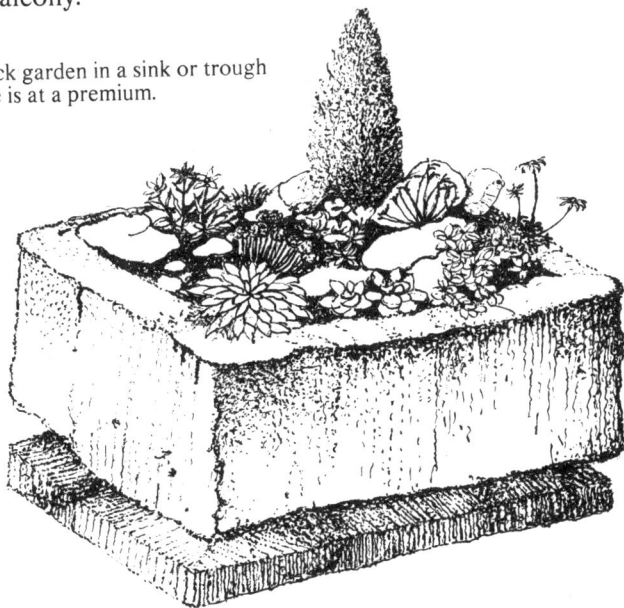

Before assembling the miniature rock garden, make a list of plants you wish to grow; it is more likely to be a success if you choose those that enjoy similar conditions, so if you decide on lime-loving plants you can use limestone rocks and an alkaline compost.

To create a sink garden you will need a container with a drainage hole at the bottom. At the bottom put a layer of crocks, rubble or coarse gravel to serve as drainage material. Over this drainage material put a layer of moss peat and cover it with a good compost, suitable for the plants you wish to grow, with some coarse gravel or sharp sand added to further aid drainage. Position the rocks, and then you are ready to plant. Choose low-growing, non-invasive, cushion-forming species. A slow-growing dwarf conifer or deciduous woody plant, like a low-growing alpine willow, can be used. A compost containing lime is suitable for saxifrages from the *Porophyllum* group, the Sedge (*Carex firma*), Sun Rose — *Helianthemum alpestre*, pinks such as *Dianthus freynii* and *D. alpinus*, Sandwort (*Arenaria tetraquetra*), all species of the genus *Edraianthus* and some low grasses or woody plants. A miniature rock garden needing a lime-free compost could include the Thrift — *Armeria caspitosa*, *Douglasia argentea*, beard tongues (*Penstemon davidsonii* and *P. rupicola*), *Lewisia cotyledon*, and *L. rediviva*, pinks — *Dianthus microlepis*, *D. glacialis*, and woody plants such as the cypress *Chamaecyparis pisifera* 'Nana'. Many other species can also be used for both types of sink garden, because the plants are usually indifferent to the pH factor (alkalinity or acidity) of the soil.

DRY STONE WALLS

A dry stone wall is a useful element to employ if your garden is situated on sloping ground and difficult to tend. You can terrace it by means of one or several dry walls. The optimum height for a dry wall is 20 to 28 in (50 to 70 cm); if the slope is steep, build several walls instead of a single high one.

The wall should be built of one type of stone, e.g. a limestone or a sandstone, not a mixture. First excavate foundations. The depth depends on the height of the wall; the higher the wall, the deeper the foundations. For walls up to 2 ft (24 in) the foundation should be about 6 in (15 cm). Rubble can be used for the foundations. The stone slabs are not bedded in mortar but fitted on top of each other and filled in with a suitable compost. The wall should be slightly trapezoidal in profile so the rain runs down the slope to moisten the plant roots without washing away the soil. Each row of stones is laid a little closer towards the slope. The face of the wall should be a little uneven to give a more natural look and to form niches and pockets for the plants. A long wall can be interrupted by a few steps or buttress to give extra support.

It is advisable and easier to plant the dry wall during the construction. This is because the plant roots can be spread out and covered with soil before the slab is laid on top; hence root damage is less likely than if the plants are poked into gaps between stones. The roots are more likely to keep moist and to establish themselves more quickly. If any planting has to be done after the wall is completed, take out some soil from the gaps between the stones and gently position the plant in the depression of moist soil. Cover the root ball with more moist soil and press it into place.

There is a wide choice of plants for the dry wall no matter how it is oriented, although south-eastern or south-western exposure is best. You can use the Chalk Plant (*Gypsophila repens*), Phlox (*Phlox subulata*), Chickwed (*Cerastium tomentosum*), various species of stonecrop, houseleek, alyssum and edraianthus (*Sedum, Sempervivum, Alyssum, Edraianthus*) and many other plants in a dry wall exposed to the sun. A shaded dry wall or one that faces north is excellent for ferns and shade-loving vegetation, of which the most beautiful are the Pyrenean Primrose (*Ramonda*) and *Haberlea*. In the flowering period, the dry stone wall is covered with masses of flowers.

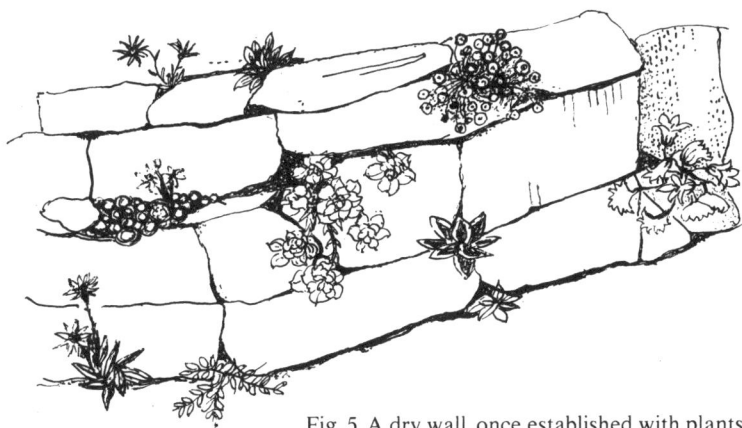

Fig. 5. A dry wall, once established with plants, is easy to maintain.

KEEPING A RECORD OF YOUR PLANTS

Some gardeners are happy with a neat garden full of flowers but show no great interest in plants as such. Others are more deeply interested in their plants. Just to know the name, colour and flowering period of their plants is not enough. They want to know where the plants come from, in what conditions they thrive. They are interested in their classification and in all the aspects of plant life. They take notes and these often develop into a reference file. If you start a file on the plants grown in your rock garden, do keep it up to date. Make out an index card for each new plant and remove or mark the cards of plants that have died. This job sounds time-consuming but it can prove both interesting and very useful. Fill in the name of the plant and any synonyms, its country of origin, ecological requirements for successful growth, type of inflorescence and time of flowering, and height, type of plant (bulbous, tuberous, perennial, shrub). Make a note of when and where you obtained the plant, when you transplanted or divided it, and any problems that have occurred. You could keep all this information in a loose-leaf folder for easier reference, if you wish.

It is easy to forget exactly where you planted your bulbs and during autumn when you prick over the ground it is easy to stab a bulb with a hand fork. It is better to mark the position of bulbs with labels rather than trust their position to memory. Labels can also be inserted beside plants that do not die down. The labels must be noticeable and made from a material which withstands the vagaries of weather, so that they do not have to be renewed too often. Plastic labels are common, and the best are those which have a plastic cover over a paper insert so the plant name can be written in biro. Those made of thin metal sheet, about ½ in (1 cm) wide and 4 to 5 in (10 to 13 cm) long are very good too. The name can be written in pencil although it may be washed off over the years; so keep a check that it is still legible. Metal labels can be inserted deep in the ground to make them less obtrusive, and they are less likely to be broken. If you do not wish to use labels, you can draw a plan of the rockery. Mark all the stones and indicate the positions of the plants by means of numbers. Then list the plants against the appropriate number.

BIBLIOGRAPHY

Alpines in Colour and Cultivation. T. C. Mansfield
Alpine and Rock Garden Plants. Anna N. Griffith
Alpines for Trouble-free Gardening. Alan Bloom
The Collingridge Guide to Collectors' Alpines. Royton E. Heath
The English Rock Garden. Reginald Farrer
Rock Plants for Small Gardens. Royton E. Heath
The Lotus Book of Water Gardening. Bill Heritage
The Quarterly Bulletins of the Alpine Garden Society

INDEX

Page numbers in *italics* refer to illustrations

Abies balsamea 12—13
Acaena 16
  argentea 16
  buchananii 16—17
  glaucophylla 16—17
  microphylla 16—17
  novae-zelandiae 16
Acantholimon 18
  glumaceum 18
  olivieri 18—19
  venustum 18
Acer palmatum 20—1
Achillea : *ageratifolia* 22—3
  chrysocoma 22—3
  filipendulina 22
  millefolium 22, 23
  serbica 22—3
Adonis : *amurensis* 24, 25
  vernalis 24—5
Aethionema : *grandiflorum*
  26—7
  rotundifolium 26—7
  warleyense 27
Allium 28
  giganteum 28
  moly 28—9
  oreophilum 28—9
Alpine Aster 52—3
Alpine Clematis 70—1
alpine meadows 214
Alpine Pink 88—9
Alpine Poppy 136—7, 215
Alpine Rose *167*
Alpine Violet 82
Alyssum 30, 217
  moellendorfianum 30
  montanum 30
  saxatile 30, *31*
  spinosum 30
American Arborvitae 192—3
Anacyclus 32
  depressus 32—3
Andrapsis 34
Androsace : *ciliata* 34
  lactea 34
  mucronifolia 35
  primuloides 34—5
  sempervivoides 35
Anemones 36—7, 158—9
Anemone : *appenina* 36—7
  blanda 36
  narcissiflora 36—7, 214
  nemorosa 36

ranunculoides 36
Antennaria : *dioica* 38—9
  plantaginifolia 39
Aquilegia : *akitensis* 40
  bertolonii 40—1
  discolor 40—1
  ecalcarata 40—1
Arabis 42
  albida 42—3
  arendsii 42
  caucasica 42
  procurrens 42
  vochinensis 42—3
Arenaria : *balearica* 45
  purpurascens 45
  tetraquetra 44, 216
Aretia 34
Armeria 46
  caespitosa 46, 216
  maritima 46
  welwitschii 47
Asperula 48
  arcadiensis 49
  hirta 49
  nitida 48
  odorata 48
Asplenium 50
  ruta-muraria 50—1
  septentrionale 50—1
  trichomanes 50
  viride 50
Aster : *alpinus* 52
  andersonii 52—3
  dumosus 52—3
Autumn Crocus 72—3

Barberry 13, 54—5
Bellflower 58—9
Berberis 54
  candidula 13, 54
  thunbergii 13, 54—5
  verruculosa 55
Blue-eyed Grass 186—7
bog gardens 214
Bristle-cone Pine *149*
brooks 212
Broom 84—5, 217
bulbs 210, 211, 218
Bulrush 213
Butomus 213
Buttercups 162

Calceolaria 56

biflora 56
  darwinii 56
  fothergillii 56
  mexicana 56
  plantaginea 56
  polyrrhiza 56, 57
  tenella 56
  umbellata 56
Campanula 58
  cochleariifolia 58
  elatines 59
  tridentata 58—9
Campions 184
Candytuft 26—7, 120—1
Carex 60
  firma 60, 214, 216
  grayi 61
  montana 60, 214
  ornithopoda 60
Cerastium 62
  alpinum 63, 162
  biebersteinii 62
  tomentosum 62, 217
Chalk Plant 112—13, 217
Chamaecyparis 13
  lawsoniana 64
  nootkatensis 64
  obtusa 13, 64
  pisifera 64—5, 216
Chamaejasme 34
Chickweed 217
Chionodoxa 66
  luciliae 66—7
  sardensis 66—7
Chrysanthemum 68
  alpinum 68—9
  arcticum 68
Cinquefoils 154
Clematis 70
  alpina 70
  macropetala 70—1
  montana 70
  tangutica 70
Cobweb Houseleek 180—1
Colchicum 72
  autumnale 72—3
  bornmuelleri 72
  hybridum 72
Columbine 40—1
construction 9—11
Corbularia 132
Corydalis : *cava* 74, 75
  cheilanthifolia 74

lutea 74
solida 74
Cotoneaster 13
dammeri 13, 77
horizontalis 13, 76, 77
microphyllus 13, 77
Cotula 78
pectinata 78—9
potentillina 78
squalida 78
Crane's-bill 110
Creeping Jenny 213
Crocus 80—1
chrysanthus 80
speciosus 80—1
tommasinianus 80—1
Cushion Pink 184—5
Cyclamen: coum 82—3
europaeum 82—3
hederifolium 82—3
neapolitanum 82—3
purpurascens 82
Cymbalaria saxifrages 172
Cypress 64—5, 216
Cytisus: decumbens 13, 84
85, 217
× kewensis 13
× praecox 13, 84
purpureus 13
scoparius 13, 84—5

Dactyloides saxifrages 173
Daffodils 132—3
Daisy 68—8
Daphne: arbuscula 86, 87
blagayana 86, 87
cneorum 86, 87
mezereum 86
Dianthus: alpinus 88—9, 216
glacialis 88—9, 216
subacaulis 88—9
Dog's Tooth Violet 100—1
Draba 8
alpina 90—1
bryoides 91
Dryas: drummondii 92
octopetala 92, 93
× suendermannii 92
tenella 93
dry stone walls 216—17

Eastern Hemlock 198—9
ecological factors 209—10
Edraianthus 216, 217
dalmaticus 94
dinaricus 94
graminifolius 94, 95
pumilio 94, 95
serpyllifolius 94

tenuifolius 94
Engleria saxifrages 174
Eranthis 96
cilicica 96, 97
hyemalis 96—7
Erigeron 98
alpinus 98
humilis 98, 99
leiomerus 98, 99
neglectus 98
uniflorus 98
Erythronium 100
dens-canis 100—1
oregonum 100, 101
revolutum 100
Euaizoonia saxifrages 172
Eunomia rotundifolia 26
Euonymus fortunei 217
Euphorbia 102
capitulata 102, 103
epithymoides 102
myrsinites 102, 103
polychroma 102
European Bloody Crane's Bill
111
Evergreen Candytuft 120, 121

Ferns 50—1, 142
Festuca 104, 214
cinerea 104—5
gigantea 104
punctoria 104, 105
scoparia 104, 105
Field Anemone 158
Fingered Fumitory 74
Fleabane 98—9
Flowering Onion 28—9
Flowering Rush 213
Fritillaria: meleagris 106,
214
pallidiflora 106—7
Fumitory 74—5

Garland Flower 86—7
Gentian 108
Gentiana: acaulis 108, 214
septemfida 109
sino-ornata 108
verna 8, 108—9, 109, 162,
214
Geranium: dalmaticum 110
sanguineum 111
sessiliflorum 110, 111
tuberosum 110
Glacier Crowfoot 162
Gladiolus 214
Globe Flower 196, 214
Glory-of-the-snow 66—7
Golden Garlic 28—9

Grape Hyacinth 130—1.
Grasses 214
gravel 8
Groundsel Senecio 182—3
Gypsophila: bungeana 113
cerastioides 113
repens 112—13, 217

Haberlea 160, 161, 217
ferdinandi-coburgi 161
rhodopensis 161
habitat 209—10
Hairy Alpine Rose 167
Hart's Tongue Fern 142
Hawkweed 118
Hedera helix 82
Hedraeanthus 94
Helianthemum: alpestre 114,
115, 215, 216
hybridum 114, 115
nummularium 114—15
oelandicum 114
Helichrysum 116
arenarium 116, 117
marginatum 116
milfordiae 12, 116
selago 116, 117
Heliosperma alpina 213
Herringbone Cotoneaster
76—7
Hieracium: auranticum 119
pilosella 119
villosum 118
Hinoki Cypress 64—5
Hollow Fumitory 74
Hoop-petticoat Daffodil 132,
133
Horned Violet 206
Houseleeks 180, 217

Iberis 120
saxatilis 120
sempervirens 120, 121
Iceland Poppy 136
Iridodictyum 122
Iris 124—5
arenaria 124, 125
cristata 124
danfordiae 122—3
graminea 124, 125
lacustris 124—5
pumila 124, 125
reticulata 122, 123, 132

Jankaea 160
Japanese Maple 20—1
Jovibarba 180
sobolifera 180, 181
Juniperus: chinensis 126, 127

communis 12, 126—7
conferta 217
procumbens 12
squamata 126
virginiana 126, *127*
Juno 122

Kabschia saxifrages 174
Knotweed 152

labelling 218
Lebanon Candytuft 27
Lewisia: *brachycalyx* 128
columbiana 129
cotyledon 128—9, 216
nevadensis 128
rediviva 128, 216
Limonium 18
London Pride 172
Lysimachia nummularia 213

Maidenhair Spleenwort
50—1
maintenance 210—11
Maples 20
materials 8
Mezereon 86
Milfoil 22—3
Milkwort 102—3
miniature gardens 215—16
Moss Campion 184—5
Moss Pink 140
Mossy Saxifrages *173*
Mountain Alyssum 30—1
Mountain Avens 13, 92—3
Mountain Buttercup 162
Mountain Cat's Ear 38—9
Mountain Everlasting 38—9
Mountain Pine 148
Mountain Soldanella 188—9
Mouse-eared Chickweed
62—3
Mouse-ear Hawkweed *119*
Muscari:
armeniacum 130, *131*
botryoides 130—1

Narcissus 132, 214,
bulbocodium 132, *133*
cyclamineus 132
rupicola 132, *133*
Nymphaea pygmaea 213

Onion, Flowering 28—9
orchids 8, 214
Oxalis 134
acetosella 134
corniculata 134
enneaphylla 134

inops 134, *135*
lactea *135*

Papaver: *alpinum* 136—7,
215
nudicaule 136
pyrenacium 136, *137*
Pasque Flower 158
paths 10, 211—12
Penstemon: *cardwelii* *139*
caespitosus 138
hirsutus 139
pinifolius 138, *139*
pubescens *139*
Phlox 140
amoena *141*
divaricata 140
douglasii 140, *141*
subulata 140, 217
Phyllitis scolopendrium
142—3
Physoplexis comosa 144
Phyteuma 144
comosum 144
hemisphaericum 144, *145*
orbiculare 144, *145*
Picea: *abies* 146, *147*
glauca 12, 13, 146, *147*
pungens 146, *147*
Pines 148
Pink Cinquefoil 154
Pinks 88, 216
Pinus: *aristata* 148, *149*
cembra 148
leucodermis 148
montana 148
mugo 12, 148
nigra 148
peuce 148
sylvestris 148
strobus 148
Plantago 56
Pleione: *bulbocodioides*
150—1
formosana 150, 151
Polygonum 152
affine 152—3
bistorta 152
capitatum 152
vacciniifolium 152, *153*
viviparum 152, *153*
pools 212—14
Poppies 136—7
Porophyllum saxifrages 174,
216
Potentilla 154—5
ambigua 154—5
fruticosa 154
nepalensis *155*

nitida 154
Prickly Thrift 18—19
Primula: *auricula* 156—7
florindae 156
marginata *157*
minima 156
Pseudoprimula 34
Ptilotrichum spinosum 30
Pulsatilla 158
pratensis 158—9
vernalis 158—9
vulgaris 158
Pyrenean Primrose 160—1,
217

Ragwort 182—3
Ramonda 160, 217
myconi 160, *161*
nathaliae 160
serbica 160
Rampion 144
Ranunculus: *alpestris*
162—3
glacialis 162, *163*
montanus 162—3
Raoulia 164
australis 164—5
glabra 164
lutescens 164—5
subsericea 164—5
records, keeping 218
Reedmace 213
Reticulate Willow 168
Rhododendron, 8, 13
ferrugineum 167
hirsutum 166, *167*
impeditum 166—7
'Praecox' 166
Ribgrass 39, 56
Robertsonia saxifrages 172
Rock Cress 42—3
Rockfoil 172—3
Rock Rose, Common
114—15
Rock Soapwort 171
Round-headed Rampion 144

Salix: *alpina* *169*
myrsinites *169*
reticulata 13, 168
serpyllifolia 168, *169*
sandwort 44—5, 216
Saponaria: *caespitosa* 170
ocymoides *171*
× *olivana* 170—1
pumila 170
Sarothamnus scoparius 84
Satin Flower 186—7
Saxifrages 172—3, 174—5,
216

Saxifraga : *aizoon* 172
  × *boydii* 174
  callosa 172
  cochlearis 172
  cotyledon 172
  cymbalaria 172
  grisebachii 174
  hostii 172
  lingulata 172
  longifolia 172
  paniculata 172
  umbrosa 172
Scilla : *autumnalis* 176
  bifolia 176—7
  hispanica 176—7
  pratensis 176
  siberica 176—7
Scirpus 213
Scotch Pine 148
scree beds 214—15
Sea Campion 184
Sea Pink 46
Sedge 60—1, 216
Sedum : *acre* 178
  album *179*
  spathulifolium 179
  spurium 179
Semiaquilegia ecalcarata 40
Sempervivum :
  arachnoideum 180, 217
  montanum 180, *181*
  soboliferum 180, *181*
Senecio 182
  abrotanifolius 182—3
  incanus 182, *183*
  uniflorus 182
Silene : *acaulis* 184
  hookeri 184
  maritima 184
  schafta 184—5
  schmuckeri 184
Silver Saxifrage 172

sink gardens 215—16
Sisyrinchium 186
  angustifolium 186
  bellum 186
  californicum 186, *187*
  striatum 186
site 8—9
Slipper Flower 56—7
Snake's Head Fritillary
  106—7
snow 209
Snow-in-summer 62—3
Soapwort 170—1
soil 8, 209
Soldanella 188
  minima 189
  montana 188
  pusilla 188, *189*
Sorrels 134
Sowbread 82—3
Spanish Bluebell 176
Speedwell 204
Spindle 217
Spring Adonis 24—5
Spring Anemone 158
Spruces 146
Spurge 102—3
Squills 176
steps 10, 211—12
Stonecrop 178—9, 217
Store Cress *27*
Sun Rose 215, 216
Sweet Violet 207

Taxus baccata 190, *191*
Thrift 46—7, 216
Thuja 13
  occidentalis 192
Thymus : × *citriodorus* 194
  doerfleri 195
  serpyllum 194
Toadflax 215

Trollius : *acaulis* 196
  × *cultorum* 196
  europaeus 196—7, 214
  pumilus 196
Tsuga 13, 198
  canadensis 13, 198—9
Tulipa : *aucheriana* 200—1
  tarda 200—1
  urumiensis *200—1*
Two-leaved Squill 176

Valeriana 202
  montana 203
  supina 202
  tripteris 202, *203*
Veronica 204
  filiformis 204
  incana 204—5
  prostrata 204—5
  surculosa 204
Viola 206
  biflora 206
  cornuta 206
  lutea 206
  odorata 206, *207*
  palustris 207

Wahlenbergia 94
walls 216—17
water 209, 210, 212—13
White Pine 148
White Spruce 146
Wild Thyme 194—5
Willows 13, 168—9
Winter Aconite 96—7
Woodruff 48—9
Wood Sorrel 134—5

Yarrow 22—3
Yellow Whitlow Grass 90—1
Yellow Wood Violet 206
Yew 190—1